P9-BYD-643

The Dividend Rich Investor

Building Wealth with High-Quality, Dividend-Paying Stocks

Joseph Tigue
Joseph Lisanti

McGraw-Hill

New York   San Francisco   Washington, D.C.   Auckland   Bogotá
Caracas   Lisbon   London   Madrid   Mexico City   Milan
Montreal   New Delhi   San Juan   Singapore
Sydney   Tokyo   Toronto

McGraw-Hill

A Division of The **McGraw·Hill** Companies

Copyright © 1997 by The McGraw-Hill Companies, Inc. All rights reserved. Printed in the United States of America. Except as permitted under the United States Copyright Act of 1976, no part of this publication may be reproduced or distributed in any form or by any means, or stored in a data base or retrieval system, without the prior written permission of the publisher.

1   2   3   4   5   6   7   8   9   0   DOC/DOC   9   0   1   0   9   8   7   6

ISBN 0-07-064639-2

The editors for this book were David Conti and Allyson Arias, the editing supervisor was Fred Dahl, and the production supervisor was Pamela Pelton. It was set in Caslon 540 by Inkwell Publishing Services.

Printed and bound by R. R. Donnelley & Sons Company.

McGraw-Hill books are available at special quantity discounts to use as premiums and sales promotions, or for use in corporate training programs. For more information, please write to the Director of Special Sales, McGraw-Hill, 11 West 19th Street, New York, NY 10011. Or contact your local bookstore.

This publication is designed to provide accurate and authoritative information in regard to the subject matter covered. It is sold with the understanding that the publisher is not engaged in rendering legal, accounting, or other professional service. If legal advice is required, the services of a competent professional person should be sought.
—from a declaration of principles jointly adopted by a committee of the American Bar Association and a committee of publishers

Contents

Contents

Contents

Foreword

Investors these days like having things done for them. The mutual fund manager selects the stocks and times the purchases, after the 401(k) plan automatically deducts the money from the investors' paychecks.

Now, if you do buy stocks directly, the companies in which you have an ownership interest are telling you that they know better what to do with the fruits of your investment than you do. The latest trend among U.S. corporations is to pay out as little as possible to you in dividends and instead use the cash as *they* see fit. The payout ratio—dividends as a percentage of earnings—has fallen to one of the lowest levels in history. And that's not because the economy is on the brink of disaster, so that companies have to hoard cash. Profits are running at record levels.

If you've wondered why stock yields are so meager, a good part of the reason is low payout ratios. The other part, of course, is high stock prices. As of September 1996, the yield of the S&P 500 index was only about half the average of 4.4% in the 70 years from 1926 to 1995. It had been under 3% since October 1992, or for three and a half years. Before that, the longest continuous period of sub-3% yields was January 1972 through May 1973, or one and a third years.

To be fair, by retaining a huge part of its earnings, the corporation you invest in often does have your best interests in mind. It's trying to enhance the value of your shares through what it regards as an attractive opportunity to invest in the company itself or in the company's stock in the open market (share buybacks).

A low payout policy is also good for corporate managers. They benefit, as you would, if the shares rise in price, thanks to options and executive compensation tied to stock performance. They also love the flexibility of being able to deploy corporate earnings when and how they choose—buying in shares, paying down debt, building plants, making acquisitions, and the like.

To a large degree, however, what the company is offering you, the shareholder, is a promise. It is saying it will invest profitably for you money that would otherwise go straight into your pocket. That's worked well as the stock market has soared. As you've watched the prices of your shares climb, you've been able to tell yourself that the dividends you've lost out on haven't been missed and that, at the same time, you've been tax-wise. (Dividends are taxed as ordinary income in the year received. Appreciation is taxed at a usually lower capital gains rate—and then only when you sell the shares.)

But don't forget the "a bird in the hand" adage. If stock prices level off or decline for a time, the dividend will prove to be your friend. Maybe you want to use dividends to pay monthly bills. Or perhaps you prefer to be the one to decide when and by how much to increase your investment in a particular company, if at all—and not leave that choice to the company. If you do want to increase your investment, generally it's as simple as enrolling in the company's dividend reinvestment plan. If you don't, you should be entitled to a reasonable and growing dividend.

The coauthors of this book, Joseph Tigue and Joseph Lisanti, have seen the investment winds shift more than a few times. They know the difference between fads and time-tested investment concepts. They are especially aware of how some big, big nest eggs have developed from years of expanding dividend income. Joe and Joe bring to this work a combined total of more than forty years of experience, much of it in researching, writing, and editing feature articles for one of the oldest and most successful investment advisory publications, Standard & Poor's *The Outlook*. They'll give you some excellent advice on how to make dividends work for you.

ARNOLD M. KAUFMAN
Editor, *The Outlook*

Acknowledgments

Although writing a book has often been described as a lonely pursuit, we have been fortunate to have a group of knowledgeable people always available to discuss various ideas and concepts that ultimately found their way into this work. We thank them for their efforts, without which this book would be poorer.

Many of our colleagues at Standard & Poor's have been generous in offering a helping hand at numerous points along the creative path: Jim Dunn and Arnold Kaufman read over the manuscript and offered helpful suggestions on how to make it better and clearer. Chris Peng worked hard, as she always does, to create the charts that grace these pages. Howard Silverblatt tweaked the vast S&P databases to provide us with numerous tables of interesting stocks. David Braverman did the pioneering work on electric utilities stocks that we built upon in Chapter 8. Carol Fitzgerald, Rick Perdew, and Richard ZainEldeen located the sometimes obscure materials that we needed to complete our research.

We would also like to thank Bruce Agostino of the New York Stock Exchange, Katrina Clay of the American Stock Exchange, Robert Cohen of First Call, Ed Keon of I/B/E/S, and Bill Wink of Nasdaq for providing information on the services available from their organizations.

Thanks to Fred Dahl for his extraordinary attention to detail in turning our manuscript into a book. A special thanks to our patient editors at McGraw-Hill, David Conti and Allyson Arias, who never once laughed at our outrageous predictions of how little time it would take to write this book.

We would also like to thank our wives, Barbara Tigue and Judith Cooperstein Lisanti, whose understanding and support made this book possible.

J.T. & J.L.
New York

Introduction

Most people have financial goals in life. Since you are reading this book, we assume you do, too. Maybe you want to set aside enough money to pay for the education of your children, or to buy a home, or to provide for a comfortable retirement. Whatever your financial goals, the dividend-based stock market strategies explained in this book can help you achieve them—slowly and steadily.

Ours is not a "get-rich-quick" approach. We won't show you how to spot hot new trends or buy shares of companies that are just going public. Instead, we'll teach you how to identify long-term (and very profitable) patterns in high-quality stocks.

Nor will we tell you how to time the stock market, because we don't believe it can be done consistently. Attempting to pick the "right" and "wrong" times to own stocks is a fool's errand: The stock market's short-term gyrations are never completely predictable. Instead, we will show you how to pick outstanding stocks that produce steady returns in both good markets and bad.

We won't tell you a thing about bonds, real estate, gold, gems, art works, or anything else people buy and sell in an attempt to make money. True, Old Master paintings sometimes appreciate faster than stocks for long periods of time. But how many people do you know who can afford to buy a Rembrandt? In the almost seven decades since 1928, no other readily available investment has beaten the gains from common stocks. And that time frame includes the Great Depression as well as the decade-long bear market that ended in 1982.

This book will provide you with the insights, guidelines, and tools you need for a lifetime of profitable stock market investing. We've even included numerous lists of stocks worth considering for your portfolio. But to use this information successfully, you must have both patience and flexibility.

Patience is, by far, more difficult. There will be times (most recently the technology bull market of 1995) when the strategies we outline will seem slow, outdated, and even irrelevant. As friends, relatives, and even the occasional cab driver boast of their prowess in picking the latest trendy stock, you will be tempted to abandon the slow-and-steady approach we advocate.

Don't. Hot stocks cool off as investors' perceptions change, and money made quickly can be lost just as rapidly.

Neither do we suggest that you should simply buy stocks from the lists in this book and hold them forever without periodic evaluation. The only constant in life is change: Companies merge, enter new businesses, exit old ones, change managements, and face new competitors every day. While we advocate long-term stock investments, we would never tell you that any stock should be a permanent part of your portfolio. You should always keep up with developments in the companies whose stocks you own. Read their annual and quarterly reports as well as a good daily or weekly summary of business news that will alert you to important developments. When the reasons you bought the stock are no longer valid, you must be flexible enough to sell.

You don't need a lot of money to begin using our strategies. Readers with limited means should consider mutual funds (see Chap. 6) and dividend reinvestment plans (Chap. 5) as ways of making modest regular investments. Also, you won't need a knowledge of higher mathematics to use this book. We've often found that the more complex the equation describing an investment, the more likely you are to lose money on it. A pencil, a note pad, and a pocket calculator are all you'll need to perform any calculation in this book.

Why Dividends Are Important

Dividends are the Rodney Dangerfield of investing: They get no respect. Not many people brag about dividend-paying stocks that they've owned for a dozen years. A regular annual return over a long period of time just doesn't seem to invite the envy of friends and relatives. But in many ways, investing in stocks that pay dividends is like betting on the tortoise in Aesop's fable. Even though the hare is faster, slow and steady wins the race.

We think that dividends, and the slow-and-steady investment philosophy that they suggest, deserve a lot of respect. Dividends are excellent tools for analyzing conservative stock investments. Growing dividends can lead you to shares of companies whose managements are confident about future earnings. Dividend yields can indicate when a stock is undervalued. And filling your portfolio with stocks that pay dividends can cut down on the overall volatility of your investment holdings.

At this point, it might be a good idea to define some of our terms. *Dividends* are the per-share cash payments that many publicly traded companies provide to their shareholders. If a company pays a dividend, you will find its annual cash payment listed in the stock tables of major newspapers under the column heading "DIV."

Some companies pay dividends in additional shares. These are called *stock dividends* in contrast to the more common cash dividends. In this book, we will be discussing dividends paid in cash, unless we indicate otherwise. Most companies pay cash dividends quarterly. But since the board of directors can vote to increase or decrease a company's dividend at any time during the year, investment professionals take the latest quarterly per-share payment and multiply that figure by four to come up with the *indicated dividend*, which is simply what you would expect to receive in payments per share of common stock in the coming year. In common usage, the term *current dividend* also means the indicated dividend. Unless we indicate otherwise, when we discuss historical dividend information in this book, we will use the actual amount paid per share during the year in question.

If a company has announced a dividend increase, that new quarterly figure will be multiplied by four to arrive at the indicated dividend. For example, in late 1994, health care company Abbott Laboratories declared a quarterly dividend of $0.19 a share, payable to its shareholders on February 15, 1995. Newspaper stock listings showed Abbott's dividend as .76, which was the indicated rate (four times the quarterly payment of 19 cents) at that time. Before Abbott paid its next shareholder dividend in May 1995, the board had voted to increase the quarterly payment to $0.21 a share. As soon as the announcement was made, newspapers began listing Abbott's dividend as .84, the new indicated rate.

People new to investing often confuse dividend and *yield*. A stock's yield, which is given as a percent, is simply its indicated dividend divided by the current price of a share. Since share prices move up and down in the stock market and change daily for most common stocks, the yield will vary much more than the dividend. Again, let's take Abbott Laboratories as an example. On March 22, 1995, Abbott's stock ended the trading day at $38 a share. Since we know that its indicated dividend on that date was $0.84, the stock's yield was 2.2%. Just about three months later, Abbott's stock closed at 42. Although the indicated dividend remained the same, the yield had fallen to 2%.

An important concept to understand is *total return*, which encompasses an investment's price change plus any income it generates. In the case of stocks, the income is from dividends. The total return from dividend-paying stocks takes on even greater importance in periods of market weakness. In 1994, the stock market ended the year slightly below where it began. Over the course of that year, the shares of personal care and household products maker Colgate-Palmolive outpaced the market by rising only 1.6%. Yet owners of Colgate stock had a total return of 3.3% in 1994, because they received dividends in addition to the increased value of their shares.

Over the last 60-odd years, the total return of stocks in general, as measured by the S&P 500 index, has been a little more than 10% annually. Dividend-paying stocks can give you a leg up on your main goal in investing: making money. If, for example, you buy a good stock that yields 5%, you're halfway to matching the market's historical performance. That's an important advantage, since most professional money managers fail to outperform the market on a consistent basis. From 1986 through 1995, only 14% of diversified equity mutual funds beat the performance of the "500," according to Morningstar, Inc., which tracks mutual fund performance.

As we said, dividends don't get much respect from the average investor. Even though picking stocks with growing dividends or above-average current dividends makes it easier to succeed at building your nest egg, most novice investors, and many professionals, ignore these payments when selecting stocks. They've been misled into thinking that investing doesn't require patience. In a world of instant gratification, many people look for a hot stock to buy today at 7 and sell in three weeks at 20. Unfortunately, such results are more often the stuff of cocktail party chatter than reality. Most investors who try their hands at hot stocks only get burned.

You Can Bank on It

Dividends, on the other hand, are real. They represent a tangible return to you, the shareholder. They are payment to you as an owner of a going business. What's more, you don't have to give up your ownership stake in a company to earn this return. In contrast, unless you want to get involved with options, the only way you can realize a return on shares that don't pay dividends is to sell them.

Dividends are money in the bank. Once you receive the check, or the credit to your brokerage account, that money is yours. It can't be taken away from you. Unrealized capital gains, however, can disappear quickly, sometimes in a single day. In bear markets, such as the long dry spell for stocks in the decade before August 1982, you may not even have any gains to lose. Dividends provide your only return when stocks are weak. See Fig. 1-1 for one of the best examples in modern times of the power of dividends to provide returns in a flat market.

As we've mentioned, stocks didn't have a great year in 1994. The S&P 500 index, which professionals use as a proxy for the general market since it represents 70% of the value of all U.S. common stocks, fell 1.5% for the year. Despite that small decline, an investor who owned an index fund that replicates the "500" still showed a small total return (about 1.3%, not counting the fund's expenses) because of dividend-paying stocks in the index.

The next chart (Fig. 1-2) shows the price change, the annual yield, and the total return of the S&P 500 for each of the ten years ending in 1995. We assumed that you had

Figure 1-1. Effect of Dividends in a Flat Market. This chart shows the decade immediately preceding the great bull market that began in August 1982. If you had invested $100 in the stock market (as measured by the S&P 500 index) in the summer of 1972, your investment would have been worth about the same *ten years* later. But had you reinvested dividends, the value of your holdings would have been *almost 60% higher.*

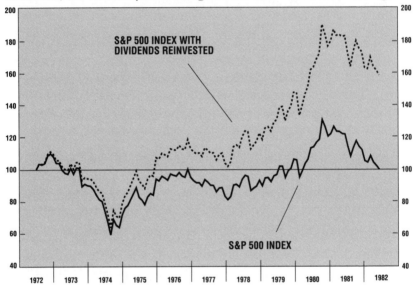

"bought" the S&P 500 at the start of each year and collected the actual dividends paid on the stocks (in proportion to their weighting in the index) throughout the year. Note the yield of the "500" in relation to its gain or loss in each of the years. In the years 1990 and 1994, the yield from dividends was the only income an investor in the market had. Over the ten-year period, the yield of the "500" averaged 3.4%, while the market posted an average price gain of 12%. In other words, cash dividends equaled 28% of the average appreciation of stocks during that period. For the

Figure 1-2. Price Change, Yield, and Total Return of S&P 500 Index. Even in a strong bull market, dividends provide a significant return. In down years, such as 1990 and 1994, they are the *only* return on your stock investments.

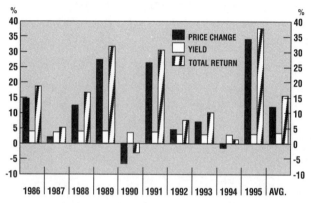

many investors who take dividends in cash, rather than reinvesting them in additional shares of a stock, this is a realistic view. If you do reinvest your dividends, as we'll discuss in Chap. 5, your returns should be greater.

True, your future dividends from common shares aren't guaranteed. Buying stocks is not the same as depositing your savings in a bank backed by federal insurance. In investing, the caveat has always been that past performance is no guarantee of future results. Just because a company has steadily paid or increased its dividend for many years does not mean that it will always do so. In May 1994, FPL Group, a Florida-based electric utility holding company, cut its annual dividend from $2.48 to $1.68 per share, even though it had increased the payment annually for the preceding forty-eight years. The news sent shock waves throughout the investment community and the company's shares plunged almost 14% on the day of the announcement.

What went unnoticed in all the furor surrounding FPL's dividend cut is how rare such an action really is. The calendar year in which FPL cut its dividend saw fifty-nine companies decrease their dividends and another seventy-seven corporations omit their dividends entirely. Compared to these 136 "unfavorable" dividend actions, there were 1,826 dividend increases reported in 1994. That makes more than thirteen increases for every omitted or decreased dividend.

And although 1994 was a good year for dividends, it was not unique. Since 1956, the average yearly ratio of dividend increases to dividend cuts and omissions has been 7.4 to 1. Only once, in 1958, did cuts and omissions exceed dividend increases.

One reason payments tend to rise rather than fall over time is that most companies that pay dividends are considered mature. While mature may be a compliment in most parts of the world, in investment circles the term often is pejorative. Aggressive investors seek out young, dynamic companies that can grow their earnings at 20%, 30%, or more each year. These companies are still building their businesses and plow back all of their earnings into expanding operations. In contrast, so the theory goes, mature companies can't get a good enough return on further investments in their traditional businesses, so they pay out a large part of their profits to shareholders in the form of dividends.

Of course, reality clashes with this overly simplified division between growing companies and mature ones.

General Electric is on almost everyone's list of dynamic, growing companies. The diversified giant operates in twelve major business lines and is an industry leader in most of them. Its products range from high-tech jet aircraft engines to mundane light bulbs. In the ten years ended 1995, GE posted a compound annual per-share earnings gain of 11.7%. Not bad for a company that has paid a dividend since 1899 and increased it every year since 1975. And General Electric is far from alone. As we'll show you in the chapters that follow, you don't have to invest in has-been companies to benefit from a strategy that emphasizes dividend growth.

Dividends Provide Stability

For as long as anyone can remember, investors have intuitively understood that dividend-paying stocks provide a higher degree of price stability than non-dividend-paying issues. When the market declines, as it does periodically, most stocks will drop in value. In these corrections, investors tend to hold on to stocks that will provide them with another cash payment in a few months and dump those whose only attraction is that they are expected to go up in price. In other words, stocks that pay dividends have less volatility than those that don't. The flip side of this statement is that in strong bull markets, stocks that pay dividends are not the highest fliers. But remember, the tortoise, over time, beats the hare!

The protective aspects of dividend-paying stocks were apparent in the October 19, 1987 stock market crash.

In the space of that one day, the widely followed Dow Jones Industrial Average (composed of thirty major blue chip stocks) fell 508 points, or 22.6%. That surpassed the infamous October 1929 crash, in which the Dow fell 12.8% in a day, to become the largest one-day decline in the history of the modern stock market.

A major academic study of the October 1987 event showed that stocks with the highest yields prior to the crash fell 21.2%, while stocks that paid no dividends tumbled 32%. Dr. Avner Arvel, professor of finance at Cornell University, and his colleagues Steven Carvell and Erik Postnieks, studied the price action of 2,000 stocks in the 1987 crash and reported their results in the May/June 1988 issue of *Harvard Business Review*. The stocks in their study included issues listed on the New York Stock Exchange and the American Stock Exchange or traded in the Nasdaq over-the-counter market, and the authors looked at these issues from several perspectives, including dividend yield.

Admittedly, a drop of "only" 21% in a single day is nothing to cheer about. But consider two hypothetical portfolios, one containing the top dividend payers and the other the non-payers. Each portfolio is worth $10,000 prior to the 1987 crash. Following the drop, the dividend-paying portfolio would have been worth $1,080 more than the portfolio that didn't pay dividends. As Dr. Arvel and his colleagues noted, "When the market environment is very uncertain, a bird in the hand is worth more than two in the bush."

This study of the 1987 crash also divided the 2,000-stock sample by industry group. It should not come as a surprise that the best-performing industry group during the crash was electric utilities. Those stocks, usually among the highest-yielding common stocks in the market, fell only 10.5%.

The Tax Question

Investment advisors who favor stocks that don't pay dividends usually like to bring up the subject of taxes. They note with some glee that, under current law, capital gains are taxed at a maximum of 28% while dividends are treated as ordinary income. This is an argument that nobody can refute. Under the U.S. tax system, capital gains can be taxed at a lower rate than dividends. But the real question is whether you will pay a higher rate on dividend income. Internal Revenue Service statistics show that more than 90% of individual tax filers pay a marginal rate of 28% or less. For the 1995 tax year, a married couple filing a joint return needed taxable income (that's income after deducting items such as mortgage interest, real estate taxes, and state and local income taxes) that exceeded $94,250 before they paid more than 28% of each additional dollar earned in federal income taxes. The 28% bracket for singles ended at $56,550 in 1995.

But let's assume that you are in the next higher tax bracket. Married couples who filed joint returns for tax year 1995 paid 31% on marginal taxable income up to $143,600; for singles, the 31% bracket ended at $117,950. For these people, the difference in taxes between $100 in dividend income and $100 in capital gains income was a mere $3. We think that for people in the 31% tax bracket, the lower volatility of dividend-paying stocks, and the leg up they provide in reaching investment goals, are worth the $3.

But what if you are in the 36% or even the top 39.6% bracket? Paying more in taxes is never fun, but you should not eliminate dividend payers from your investment portfolio. Remember, a dividend paid to you is real; capital gains remain potential until you sell the shares. Also, as we have noted, these more conservative dividend-paying issues can provide needed stability to your assets. They also make excellent choices for self-directed tax-deferred retirement accounts. More on that in Chap. 5.

Summing Up

1. *A good dividend-paying stock will give you a leg up on your investment goals.*

2. *Dividends allow you to realize a return on your stock investment without giving up ownership.*

3. *Once paid, the dividend is yours to keep.*

4. *Although dividends are not guaranteed, far more companies raise payments than cut them.*

5. *Dividend-paying stocks provide greater stability in market downturns.*

6. *For most people, taxes on dividends and those on capital gains are the same.*

What to Look for in a Dividend-Paying Stock

The novice investor looking for an income stock often starts and ends the search by seeking out the highest-yielding stocks. Wrong! Heed the hoary advice: If it looks too good to be true, it probably is.

A stock with a mouthwatering yield may well be under water in a matter of months. Never buy a stock on the basis of yield alone. A well-above-average yield means that the stock price is depressed either because earnings have been disappointing or there's some adverse news about to be announced. The high yield thus could signal either a dividend cut or dividend omission somewhere down the line.

Examples abound: IBM yielded a lofty 10% (vs. a 2.9% yield on the S&P 500 index) in January 1993, less than a month before the company announced a 55% cut in the dividend. In the late 1980s, many banks also sported juicy yields just before the real estate market crashed and they were forced to write off sizable loans. These writeoffs resulted in declining profits and wholesale dividend reductions or omissions.

Electric utilities, too, were returning extremely high yields in the mid-1980s when many of their nuclear plants were in trouble. Following the infamous Three Mile Island nuclear plant accident in early 1979, the federal Nuclear Regulatory Commission became a more vigilant watchdog, mandating expensive safety measures for nuclear plant construction. That led to huge cost overruns on the plants, while at the same time, electricity demand was falling due mainly to conservation efforts. Plant cancellations became the order of the day, which depressed earnings and resulted in widespread unfavorable dividend actions.

More recently, Crown American Realty, a real estate investment trust (REIT), yielded more than 11% in early July 1995, compared with a then more typical 6.5% for a REIT issue. In August, Crown announced a quarterly loss and slashed the annual dividend 43%, to $0.80 from $1.40.

How to Avoid Clinkers

To avoid situations like those cited above, your first step should be to check the yields of stocks in the same industry as the issue you're thinking of buying. You can do this by consulting *Standard & Poor's Analysts' Handbook*

Monthly Supplement, found in many libraries, which contains dividend yields of all industry groups. *The Value Line Investment Survey* is also a good source to research yields. If you find that the industry average yield is considerably lower than that of your buy candidate, steer clear, unless you're willing to take on above-average risk. We'll discuss when to break this rule in Chap. 8.

You will actually fare better by buying lower-yielding stocks that have a long history of boosting dividends each year. Although such companies typically don't declare large increases, when dividend payments are hiked regularly, the yield on your original investment can climb dramatically over time. Let's look again at Abbott Laboratories. If you had bought the stock of this major diversified health care company in 1985 at a median price of 7 (adjusted for stock splits), you would have received a dividend of $0.17, for a yield of 2.4%. Based on the 1995 indicated annual rate of $0.84, however, you would be getting a return of 12% on your 1985 cost. At the same time, the shares have appreciated over 470%. We'll have more to say on this strategy in Chap. 3.

Table 2-1 lists companies that have increased their dividends in each of the ten years from 1986 to 1995. Each of the stocks has outpaced by a wide margin the 80% increase in dividends posted by the benchmark S&P 500 index over the last decade. In addition, each of the stocks more than doubled dividend payments during the same 10 years. Top honors go to Federal National Mortgage (Fannie Mae), which paid $0.0533 annually in 1985 and $2.72 ten years later, for a gain of more than 5,000%.

Table 2-1. Dividend Increase Champions

Company	Ticker	Industry	10-year Div. Increase %
Federal National Mortgage	FNM	Financial Services	5003.2
Franklin Resources	BEN	Financial Services	2650.0
LESCO Inc.	LSCO	Lawn Care	2339.0
Student Loan Marketing	SLM	Financial Services	2122.2
Raymond James Financial	RJF	Financial Services	1457.4
CORUS Bankshares	CORS	Financial Services	1233.3
ALLIED Group	ALGR	Financial Services	1175.8
Wal-Mart Stores	WMT	Retail	1119.5
Brady (W.H.) Cl. "A"	BRCOA	Adhesives	1101.2
Arnold Industries	AIND	Trucking	1000.0
Circuit City Stores	CC	Retail	971.4
Electronic Data Systems	EDS	Computer Services	967.8
Sysco Corp.	SYY	Distribution	940.0
Cintas Corp.	CTAS	Uniforms	900.0
Gallagher (Arthur J.)	AJG	Financial Services	852.4
Washington Federal	WFSL	Financial Services	799.7
TCA Cable TV	TCAT	Media	775.0
Philip Morris Cos.	MO	Tobacco	731.3
Archer-Daniels-Midland	ADM	Agribusiness	723.0
Merck & Co.	MRK	Health Care	665.3
Roto-Rooter, Inc.	ROTO	Consumer Services	655.6
Hach Co.	HACH	Instruments	633.9
UST, Inc.	UST	Tobacco	588.4
Hasbro, Inc.	HAS	Toys	540.0
Ennis Business Forms	EBF	Specialty Printing	532.9

Company	Ticker	Industry	10-year Div. Increase %
Eaton Vance	EV	Financial Services	518.2
Health Care Property Investors	HCP	REIT	502.7
Cooper Tire & Rubber	CTB	Tires	500.0
Valspar Corp.	VAL	Chemicals	500.0
Technalysis Corp.	TECN	Computer Services	493.7
Albertson's, Inc.	ABS	Retail	462.2
Schering-Plough	SGP	Health Care	452.4
Wausau Paper Mills	WSAU	Forest Products	451.2
PepsiCo, Inc.	PEP	Food/Beverage	449.8
Flightsafety International	FSI	Business Services	449.0
Hartford Steam Boiler Insurance	HSB	Financial Services	444.5
Golden West Financial	GDW	Financial Services	442.9
Medtronic, Inc.	MDT	Health Care	433.9
SunTrust Banks	STI	Financial Services	433.3
Pioneer Group	PIOG	Financial Services	424.9
Cardinal Health	CAH	Distribution	415.0
Bard (C.R.)	BCR	Health Care	412.0
Bemis Co.	BMS	Packaging	412.0
State Street Boston	STT	Financial Services	409.9
Fifth Third Bancorp	FITB	Financial Services	404.4
Loctite Corp.	LOC	Chemicals	400.0
Brown-Forman Cl "B"	BF.B	Food/Beverage	398.1
Abbott Laboratories	ABT	Health Care	397.9
Rubbermaid, Inc.	RBD	Household Products	397.8
Automatic Data Processing	AUD	Computer Services	392.3

Table 2-1. Dividend Increase Champions *(cont'd)*

Company	Ticker	Industry	10-year Div. Increase %
National Penn Bancshares	NPBC	Financial Services	390.1
Anheuser-Busch Cos.	BUD	Food/Beverage	380.2
Disney (Walt) Co.	DIS	Leisure	380.0
ConAgra, Inc.	CAG	Food/Beverage	373.8
Temple-Inland	TIN	Forest Products	368.7
Nordstrom, Inc.	NOBE	Retail	354.5
Synovus Financial	SNV	Financial Services	352.3
First Empire State	FES	Financial Services	348.0
First Michigan Bank	FMBC	Financial Services	344.7
Hillenbrand Industries	HB	Caskets/Locks/ Hospital Beds	344.4
Hormel Foods	HRL	Food/Beverage	344.4
Campbell Soup	CPB	Food/Beverage	341.6
Wilmington Trust Corp.	WILM	Financial Services	336.4
American International Group	AIG	Financial Services	334.8
Associated Banc-Corp	ASBC	Financial Services	333.4
Nucor Corp.	NUE	Steel	330.8
Family Dollar Stores	FDO	Retail	330.1
Tootsie Roll Industries	TR	Food/Beverage	326.6
Firstar Corp.	FSR	Financial Services	325.9
Great Lakes Chemical	GLK	Chemicals	318.2
Johnson & Johnson	JNJ	Health Care	314.2
Block (H & R)	HRB	Consumer Services	312.9

Company	Ticker	Industry	10-year Div. Increase %
Northern Trust	NTRS	Financial Services	310.3
Teleflex, Inc.	TFX	Machinery/ Equipment	309.0
Kelly Services Cl. "B"	KELYB	Business Services	308.2
Baldor Electric	BEZ	Machinery/ Equipment	305.4
Legg Mason, Inc.	LM	Financial Services	302.7
Central Reserve Life	CRLC	Financial Services	300.0
Illinois Tool Works	ITW	Machinery/ Equipment	300.0
Pitney Bowes	PBI	Machinery/ Equipment	300.0
Superior Surgical	SGC	Health Care	300.0
Avery Dennison Corp.	AVY	Adhesives	287.1
Walgreen Co.	WAG	Retail	287.0
Heinz (H.J.)	HNZ	Food/Beverage	285.5
Smucker (J.M.) Cl. "A"	SJM.A	Food/Beverage	285.2
General Binding	GBND	Machinery/ Equipment	283.2
First Northern Capital	FNGB	Financial Services	282.3
Banc One Corp.	ONE	Financial Services	273.4
Cincinnati Financial	CINF	Financial Services	273.3
AFLAC, Inc.	AFL	Financial Services	272.5
Wallace Computer Services	WCS	Computer Services	272.0
Alfa Corp.	ALFA	Financial Services	270.7
Gillette Co.	G	Toiletries	269.2

Table 2-1. Dividend Increase Champions *(cont'd)*

Company	Ticker	Industry	10-year Div. Increase %
Modine Manufacturing	MODI	Machinery/ Equipment	269.2
Huntington Bancshares	HBAN	Financial Services	267.3
Liqui-Box Corp.	LIQB	Packaging	266.7
Harland (John H.)	JH	Specialty Printing	264.3
Intl Flavors & Fragrances	IFF	Chemicals	264.3
Heilig-Meyers	HMY	Retail	263.6
U.S. Bancorp	USBC	Financial Services	262.9
First Union Corp.	FTU	Financial Services	261.7
AVEMCO Corp	AVE	Financial Services	260.1
Keystone Financial	KSTN	Financial Services	260.0
Coca-Cola Co.	KO	Food/Beverage	256.9
Quaker Oats	OAT	Food/Beverage	256.2
Stanhome, Inc.	STH	Collectibles	253.3
Hannaford Bros.	HRD	Retail	252.9
Wachovia Corp.	WB	Financial Services	252.7

Although past increases can't be projected into the future, investors looking for income can use the list to pick stocks that have a strong history of dividend boosts and are therefore likely to continue. Some of those companies have paid dividends for a long stretch of time. Table 2-2 lists companies that have paid dividends for 65 years or longer.

Table 2-2. Long-term Dividend Payers. There are no guarantees in investing, but we assume that most of these companies will continue to pay dividends.

Company	Ticker	Industry	Dividend Paid Since
Bank of Boston	BKB	Financial Services	1784
Bank of New York	BK	Financial Services	1785
Fleet Financial Group	FLT	Financial Services	1791
Chase Manhattan	CMB	Financial Services	1827
Meridian Bancorp	MRDN	Financial Services	1828
Bank of Montreal	BMO	Financial Services	1829
Bank of Nova Scotia	BNS	Financial Services	1834
CoreStates Financial	CFL	Financial Services	1844
Providence Energy	PVY	Utilities	1849
Connecticut Energy	CNE	Utilities	1850
Connecticut Natural Gas	CTG	Utilities	1851
Washington Gas Light	WGL	Utilities	1852
Allmerica Property & Casualty	APY	Financial Services	1853
Bay State Gas	BGC	Utilities	1853
CINergy Corp.	CIN	Utilities	1853
U.S. Trust	USTC	Financial Services	1854
Toronto-Dominion Bank	TD	Financial Services	1857
Berkshire Gas	BGAS	Utilities	1858
Star Banc Corp.	STB	Financial Services	1863
First of America Bank	FOA	Financial Services	1864
CT Financial Services	CFS	Financial Services	1865
PNC Bank Corp.	PNC	Financial Services	1865
CIGNA Corp.	CI	Financial Services	1867
American Express	AXP	Financial Services	1870
Crestar Financial	CF	Financial Services	1870
Royal Bank Canada	RY	Financial Services	1870

Table 2-2. Long-term Dividend Payers *(cont'd)*

Company	Ticker	Industry	Dividend Paid Since
Hartford Steam Boiler Insurance	HSB	Financial Services	1871
St. Paul Cos.	SPC	Financial Services	1872
Boatmen's Bancshares	BOAT	Financial Services	1873
Stanley Works	SWK	Tools	1877
Cincinnati Bell	CSN	Telephone	1879
AT&T Corp.	T	Telephone	1881
BCE Inc.	BCE	Telephone	1881
Corning Inc.	GLW	Glass	1881
E'town Corp.	ETW	Utilities	1881
Exxon Corp.	XON	Oil/Gas	1882
Carter-Wallace	CAR	Health Care	1883
Consolidated Edison	ED	Utilities	1885
Lilly (Eli)	LLY	Health Care	1885
UGI Corp.	UGI	Utilities	1885
United Water Resources	UWR	Utilities	1886
AlliedSignal Inc.	ALD	Auto Parts	1887
Equitable of Iowa	EIC	Financial Services	1889
Aquarion Co.	WTR	Utilities	1890
Boston Edison	BSE	Utilities	1890
Canadian Imperial Bank	CM	Financial Services	1890
Unicom Corp.	UCM	Utilities	1890
Imperial Oil Ltd.	IMO	Oil/Gas	1891
Procter & Gamble	PG	Household Products	1891
Southern New England Telecommunications	SNG	Telephone	1891
Morgan (J.P.)	JPM	Financial Services	1892
Times Mirror "A"	TMC	Publishing	1892

Company	Ticker	Industry	Dividend Paid Since
Westvaco Corp.	W	Forest Products	1892
Coca-Cola Co.	KO	Food/Beverage	1893
Amoco Corp.	AN	Oil/Gas	1894
First Merchants Corp.	FRME	Financial Services	1894
Colgate-Palmolive	CL	Household Products	1895
First Tennessee National	FTEN	Financial Services	1895
Mellon Bank Corp.	MEL	Financial Services	1895
Northern Trust	NTRS	Financial Services	1896
General Mills	GIS	Food/Beverage	1898
Springs Industries "A"	SMI	Textiles	1898
Bancorp Hawaii	BOH	Financial Services	1899
General Electric	GE	Diversified	1899
PPG Industries	PPG	Chemicals	1899
U.S. Bancorp	USBC	Financial Services	1899
Washington Water Power	WWP	Utilities	1899
Bristol-Myers Squibb	BMY	Health Care	1900
TECO Energy	TE	Utilities	1900
Union Pacific	UNP	Transportation	1900
United Illuminating	UIL	Utilities	1900
Church & Dwight	CHD	Household Products	1901
Hawaiian Electric Industries	HE	Utilities	1901
Johnson Controls	JCI	Automated Controls	1901
Norfolk Southern	NSC	Transportation	1901
Pfizer, Inc.	PFE	Health Care	1901
Alexander & Baldwin	ALEX	Transportation	1902
Campbell Soup	CPB	Food/Beverage	1902
Chubb Corp.	CB	Financial Services	1902
Eastman Kodak	EK	Photography	1902
Mobil Corp.	MOB	Oil/Gas	1902

Table 2-2. Long-term Dividend Payers *(cont'd)*

Company	Ticker	Industry	Dividend Paid Since
PECO Energy	PE	Utilities	1902
Tribune Co.	TRB	Publishing	1902
Central Hudson Gas & Electric	CNH	Utilities	1903
National Fuel Gas	NFG	Utilities	1903
NationsBank Corp.	NB	Financial Services	1903
Texaco Inc.	TX	Oil/Gas	1903
Bankers Trust NY	BT	Financial Services	1904
duPont (EI) deNemours	DD	Chemicals	1904
Potomac Electric Power	POM	Utilities	1904
Sun Co.	SUN	Oil/Gas	1904
Wiley (John) & Sons "B"	WILLB	Publishing	1904
American Brands	AMB	Diversified	1905
Handy & Harman	HNH	Metals	1905
Johnson & Johnson	JNJ	Health Care	1905
Dow Jones & Co.	DJ	Publishing	1906
Gillette Co.	G	Toiletries	1906
Home Beneficial Cl. "B"	HBENB	Financial Services	1906
Quaker Oats	OAT	Food/Beverage	1906
Union Electric	UEP	Utilities	1906
Carpenter Technology	CRS	Steel	1907
Public Service of Colorado	PSR	Utilities	1907
Public Service Enterprises	PEG	Utilities	1907
Houghton Mifflin	HTN	Publishing	1908

Company	Ticker	Industry	Dividend Paid Since
Oklahoma Gas & Electric	OGE	Utilities	1908
Orange/Rockland Utilities	ORU	Utilities	1908
UNITIL Corp.	UTL	Utilities	1908
American Electric Power	AEP	Utilities	1909
CalMat Co.	CZM	Concrete	1909
Detroit Edison	DTE	Utilities	1909
Edison International	EIX	Utilities	1909
First American Financial	FAF	Financial Services	1909
Madison Gas & Electric	MDSN	Utilities	1909
Mercantile Bancorp	MTL	Financial Services	1909
Mercantile Bankshares	MRBK	Financial Services	1909
Midwest Resources	MWR	Utilities	1909
Pacific Enterprises	PET	Utilities	1909
San Diego Gas & Electric	SDO	Utilities	1909
Baltimore Gas & Electric	BGE	Utilities	1910
Dauphin Deposit	DAPN	Financial Services	1910
Ingersoll-Rand	IR	Machinery	1910
New York State Electric & Gas	NGE	Utilities	1910
Northern States Power	NSP	Utilities	1910
State Street Boston	STT	Financial Services	1910
Donnelley (RR) & Sons	DNY	Printing	1911

Table 2-2. Long-term Dividend Payers *(cont'd)*

Company	Ticker	Industry	Dividend Paid Since
Dow Chemical	DOW	Chemicals	1911
Heinz (H.J.)	HNZ	Food/Beverage	1911
May Dept Stores	MA	Retail	1911
Summit Bancorp'n	SUBN	Financial Services	1911
Chevron Corp.	CHV	Oil/Gas	1912
Huntington Bancshares	HBAN	Financial Services	1912
Middlesex Water	MSEX	Utilities	1912
UST Inc.	UST	Tobacco	1912
DQE	DQE	Utilities	1913
Equifax Inc.	EFX	Information Serv.	1913
Hercules Inc.	HPC	Chemicals	1913
Jefferson-Pilot	JP	Financial Services	1913
LG&E Energy	LGE	Utilities	1913
Monarch Machine Tool	MMO	Machinery	1913
Wrigley, (Wm) Jr.	WWY	Food/Beverage	1913
Caterpillar Inc.	CAT	Equipment	1914
First Union Corp.	FTU	Financial Services	1914
Wilmington Trust Corp	WILM	Financial Services	1914
Essex County Gas	ECGC	Utilities	1915
General Motors	GM	Automobile	1915
Tasty Baking	TBC	Food/Beverage	1915
International Business Machines	IBM	Computers	1916
Melville Corp.	MES	Retail	1916
Minnesota Mining & Manufacturing	MMM	Diversified	1916
Sierra Pacific Resources	SRP	Utilities	1916

Company	Ticker	Industry	Dividend Paid Since
Unocal Corp.	UCL	Oil/Gas	1916
Idaho Power	IDA	Utilities	1917
Texas Utilities	TXU	Utilities	1917
Mine Safety Appliances	MNES	Equipment	1918
Pulitzer Publishing	PTZ	Publishing	1918
Union Carbide	UK	Chemicals	1918
American Home Products	AHP	Health Care	1919
Atlantic Energy	ATE	Utilities	1919
Avon Products	AVP	Toiletries	1919
Courier Corp.	CRRC	Publishing	1919
DPL Inc.	DPL	Utilities	1919
GATX Corp	GMT	Diversified	1919
Pacific Gas & Electric	PCG	Utilities	1919
CPC International	CPC	Food/Beverage	1920
Lincoln National Corp.	LNC	Financial Services	1920
CILCORP Inc.	CER	Utilities	1921
CLARCOR Inc.	CLC	Filtration Products	1921
Delmarva Power & Light	DEW	Utilities	1921
Deluxe Corp.	DLX	Printing	1921
ESELCO Inc.	EDSE	Utilities	1921
Kansas City Power & Light	KLT	Utilities	1921
Timken Co.	TKR	Bearings	1921
Alexander & Alexander Services	AAL	Financial Services	1922
Amerada Hess	AHC	Oil/Gas	1922
Bemis Co.	BMS	Packaging	1922
CSX Corp.	CSX	Transportation	1922
Chattem Inc.	CHTT	Toiletries	1922

Table 2-2. Long-term Dividend Payers *(cont'd)*

Company	Ticker	Industry	Dividend Paid Since
Houston Industries	HOU	Utilities	1922
Penney (J.C.)	JCP	Retail	1922
Scripps (E.W.) "A"	SSP	Publishing	1922
American National Insurance	ANAT	Financial Services	1923
BanPonce Corp.	BPOP	Financial Services	1923
Brown Group	BG	Shoes	1923
Cincinnati Milacron	CMZ	Machinery	1923
Eaton Corp.	ETN	Auto Parts	1923
International Multifoods	IMC	Food/Beverage	1923
Kellogg Co.	K	Food/Beverage	1923
Marsh & McLennan	MMC	Financial Services	1923
Media General Cl. "A"	MEG.A	Publishing	1923
NUI Corp.	NUI	Utilities	1923
Ohio Casualty	OCAS	Financial Services	1923
Washington National	WNT	Financial Services	1923
Savannah Foods & Industries	SFI	Agribusiness	1924
Seafield Capital Corp.	SFLD	Health Care	1924
Western Resources	WR	Utilities	1924
Arvin Industries	ARV	Auto Parts	1925
Bangor Hydro Electric	BGR	Utilities	1925
Dominion Resources	D	Utilities	1925
Fourth Financial	FRTH	Financial Services	1925
Monsanto Co.	MTC	Chemicals	1925
Pennzoil Co.	PZL	Oil/Gas	1925
Provident Life and Accident	PVB	Financial Services	1925
Sonoco Products	SON	Packaging	1925
Thiokol Corp.	TKC	Aerospace	1925

Company	Ticker	Industry	Dividend Paid Since
Waverly Inc.	WAVR	Publishing	1925
Abbott Laboratories	ABT	Health Care	1926
Becton, Dickinson	BDX	Health Care	1926
Duke Power	DUK	Utilities	1926
ENSERCH Corp.	ENS	Oil/Gas	1926
Frontier Corp.	FRO	Telephone	1926
Greif Brothers Cl. "A"	GBC	Shipping Containers	1926
Household International	HI	Financial Services	1926
IWC Resources Corp.	IWCR	Utilities	1926
Olin Corp.	OLN	Chemicals	1926
Owens & Minor	OMI	Health Care	1926
Protective Life Corp.	PL	Financial Services	1926
Warner-Lambert	WLA	Health Care	1926
Archer-Daniels-Midland	ADM	Agribusiness	1927
Atlantic Richfield	ARC	Oil/Gas	1927
Banta Corp.	BNTA	Packaging	1927
Fleming Cos.	FLM	Distribution	1927
Freeport McMoRan	FTX	Chemicals	1927
Georgia-Pacific	GP	Forest Products	1927
Northeast Utilities	NU	Utilities	1927
Rohm & Haas	ROH	Chemicals	1927
Standard Register	SREG	Business Forms	1927
Universal Corp.	UVV	Tobacco	1927
Eastern Utilities Associates	EUA	Utilities	1928
Honeywell, Inc.	HON	Automated Controls	1928
Hormel Foods	HRL	Food/Beverage	1928
Nalco Chemical	NLC	Chemicals	1928
Philip Morris Cos.	MO	Tobacco	1928
American General	AGC	Financial Services	1929

Table 2-2. Long-term Dividend Payers *(cont'd)*

Company	Ticker	Industry	Dividend Paid Since
American Maize-Products "A"	AZE.A	Food/Beverage	1929
Beneficial Corp.	BNL	Financial Services	1929
Briggs & Stratton	BGG	Engines	1929
First Hawaiian	FHWN	Financial Services	1929
Gannett Co.	GCI	Publishing	1929
McCormick & Co.	MCCRK	Food/Beverage	1929
Whirlpool Corp.	WHR	Appliances	1929

Payout Ratios

After you've determined that a stock's yield is not out of whack, take a look at the payout ratio. An important indicator of a company's ability to sustain good dividend growth, the payout ratio is simply the dividend expressed as a percentage of earnings, usually projected current-year profits. The Institutional Brokers Estimate System, known on Wall Street as I/B/E/S (pronounced "eye-bess") carries consensus earnings estimates for more than 5,000 U.S. and Canadian companies. Your stockbroker should have access to I/B/E/S or a competing estimate service. (See Appendix A for other information sources.) Stocks with a low payout ratio, say below 50%, have more room to increase their dividends. The payout ratio can also serve as a good gauge of growth stocks. Any issue that has increased its dividend by several hundred percent over a decade and still has a payout ratio under 50% has demonstrated strong earnings progress.

Cash Flow

Another helpful tool to determine whether a company's dividend is safe is cash flow. That's simply the company's net income plus depreciation and amortization. Statements of cash flow can be found after the balance sheet, toward the back of annual reports. A rule of thumb is that cash flow should be at least three times the dividend payout. Financial companies, such as banks, are the exception, since nearly all of their assets are cash. (For guidelines regarding banks see the section on Traditional Income Stocks following.)

Quality Rankings

As a quick test for a reliable income stock, you can check the quality ranking awarded by Standard & Poor's. The quality ranking measures the growth and stability of a company's earnings and dividends over the past ten years. A+ is highest; A, high; A–, above average; B+, average; B, below average; B–, low; C, lowest; D, in reorganization; NR, not ranked. Quality rankings are not intended to predict stock price movements. The rankings are listed in *Standard & Poor's Stock Guide*, which can be found in the business section of many libraries. Value Line's safety rankings are also a good guide.

Basics Worth Checking

As with any stock you are considering, you should check a dividend-paying equity's price-earnings ratio (P/E) against the P/E ratios of others in its industry. The P/E ratio is the most widely used tool for evaluating stocks since it quickly shows how much investors are willing to pay for each dollar of a company's earnings. Be sure you are comparing apples to apples: Some investors calculate P/E ratios using earnings of the most recent twelve months; others use estimated earnings.

P/Es generally are higher when inflation and interest rates are low. That's because low inflation means profits are the result of underlying business conditions and not simply the result of rising selling prices. A stock that sports a P/E ratio much higher than those of its competitors demands closer inspection. A high P/E (based on trailing profits) could indicate that the company has had recent earnings problems. When it's calculated on estimated earnings, a high P/E might mean that investors are bidding up the shares because of the company's strong growth prospects. Or a high P/E could simply mean a stock is temporarily overvalued. Check the stock's P/E range over the last five years to help you evaluate it.

While lower-than-average P/E multiples can signal attractive buys, they don't always. Cyclical stocks (those whose fortunes are more closely tied to economic cycles, such as chemicals and steel) often sell at low P/E multiples when investors believe that their peak profits for a given cycle are near.

Traditional Income Stocks

Electric and gas utilities, banks, and real estate investment trusts (REITs) are higher-yielding stocks that are attractive for income investors. You should keep in mind that all of these groups are sensitive to interest rates.

High interest rates cut into the profits of the utilities, since they need a large amount of capital to run operations and thus borrow heavily. Banks suffer in a high interest-rate environment because of a narrowing of their net interest margins (the spread between the cost of funds and the rate charged for loans). Margins can be squeezed because of the lag between the time that rates on deposits increase and the time that various assets, including loans, are repriced. Also, high interest rates reduce the value of a bank's fixed-rate (bond) portfolio. When interest rates rise, older bonds fall in price so that their yields move up to match the higher yield of new bonds. Conversely, when interest rates fall, older bonds rise in value. As a result, when rates climb, banks have to reposition their portfolios to account for the reduced valuations and often incur charges against profits as a result.

REITs' earnings are affected by high rates because their borrowing costs for property purchases increase. At the same time, REIT issues are regarded as bond substitutes, or yield plays. Since bonds trade primarily based on interest rate movements, REIT stocks do also. When interest rates rise, REITs, like bonds, generally drop in value, and when rates decline, the stocks typically advance. All of these groups, in fact, compete with fixed-income investments.

Following is an overview of traditional income groups. We'll tell you what to look for in each industry to assure you're picking the right stocks.

Electric Utilities

Stocks of electric utilities have been perhaps the number one haven for equity investors seeking income. The group pays out a large part of its earnings in dividends, and a good many of the companies' profits and cash flow are healthy enough to support yearly dividend hikes—increases that, in some cases, have managed to keep up with inflation over time.

As with any industry, however, selectivity is always in order. As mentioned earlier, earnings and dividends of many of the utilities in the mid-1980s were adversely affected by nuclear generating plant problems. More recently, investors have been concerned over increasing industry competition and greater environmental regulations.

The Energy Policy Act of 1992 promotes competition in the electric generation market and mandates wholesale transmission access. A utility may soon be required to allow its transmission facilities to be used for transactions between any power generating entity and another utility, which, in turn, would sell the power to the end-user.

Competition is expected to be fierce within the next five years. Discounts to large industrial customers have already been seen, and utilities have been merging in order to survive in the new environment. Two of the biggest mergers announced so far are the combinations of Northern States Power with Wisconsin Energy and Baltimore Gas & Electric with Potomac Electric Power, based in Washington, D.C. With profits hard-won, utilities have had to shutter inefficient facilities, cut staff, and reduce dividends. Over the last ten years, more than two dozen electric utilities have slashed dividend payments.

In selecting electric utilities, look for: (1) an S&P quality ranking of at least B+; (2) companies whose five-year dividend growth rate has exceeded the inflation rate; and (3) a relatively modest payout ratio (dividends as a percentage of estimated current-year profits). Utilities pay out a much larger portion of their profits than other industries, but a payout ratio above 80% should set off an alarm.

Gas Utilities

Government policies to clean up the environment have brightened prospects for natural gas stocks. Natural gas is a clean-burning fuel, and demand over at least the next few years should be above the historical norm. Some natural gas distributors are expected to enhance their earnings potential by expanding into nontraditional markets, such as cogeneration, combined-cycle power generation, and natural gas vehicles.

The new markets have been spurred by the National Energy Policy Act of 1992 and the Clean Air Act amendments passed in 1990, which encourage the use of natural gas because of the abundance of U.S. supplies and the fuel's environmental advantage. Of the new markets, power generation offers the greatest boost to overall gas demand. Power generators such as electric utilities probably will displace some usage of coal and oil with natural gas. Even without the demand stimulus associated with recent legislation, gas demand growth in this market would be significant.

Some companies worth looking into are AGL Resources (formerly Atlanta Gas Light), which has paid dividends since 1939, enjoys an above-average customer growth rate and a relatively low cost structure, and is moving into unregulated businesses; Brooklyn Union Gas, which has increased its dividend in each of the past five years and has been receiving rate relief; Pacific Enterprises, which has paid dividends since 1909 and enjoys strong cash flow; and Washington Gas Light, whose dividend payments stretch back to 1852 and whose service territory is growing.

Banks

As you can see from a quick glance at Table 2-2, Long-term Dividend Payers, banks are prominent members of that group. Their dividend history generally is positive. Lately, banks have been focusing on cost controls, loan quality, and increasing non-interest income, such as trust fees and mortgage banking income, which represents a more stable source of revenues than loans. With an oversupply of banks and fewer restrictions on interstate banking, the industry has been consolidating, which has proved to be a bonanza for shareholders of some banks that have been acquired.

In deciding which bank stocks to buy, the following measures of financial condition are useful:

- *Reserve for loan losses.* In order to cover possible future loan losses, banks are required to maintain a reserve for loan losses, which appears on the balance sheet. The reserve is a set-aside that reflects management's judgment regarding the quality of its loan portfolio, and tends to rise as asset quality deteriorates. In general, the reserve for loan losses at most banks falls within a range of 0.9% to 5% of total loans outstanding. Ratios at the top end of the range indicate that the bank has a very high level of problem loans.

- *Nonperforming loans.* The level of these loans (those in which income is no longer being accrued and for which repayment has been rescheduled) is an indication of the quality of a bank's portfolio. The ratio of nonperforming loans to total loans can range upwards from 0.5%. When it exceeds 3%, it can be a cause for concern. In addition to reducing the flow of interest income, nonperforming loans represent potential charge-offs if their quality deteriorates further.

- *Capital levels.* Banks are required by regulators to maintain minimum levels of capital. In general, the higher the capital ratio, the more conservative the bank. A higher capital ratio also indicates the ability to grow, either internally or through acquisitions.

- *Liquidity.* The extent of financial leverage, or liquidity, also says something about the relative riskiness of a bank. One measure of leverage is long-term debt divided by total equity plus total debt. For banks, a debt to equity-and-debt ratio of 50% is generally the upper limit. Banks with lower levels of debt would have room to borrow, should the need arise. A low level of debt contributes to a bank's liquidity—its ability to raise funds for lending or other purposes.

Real Estate Investment Trusts

Real estate investment trusts (REITs) afford investors an indirect means of buying a pool of professionally managed real estate assets. The assets range from health care facilities and restaurants to shopping centers and office complexes. REITs are exempt from federal corporate income taxes and most state income taxes. There are five requirements that must be met in order for a venture to qualify as a REIT: (1) 95% of income must be distributed annually to shareholders in the form of dividends; (2) only a limited number of a company's properties can be sold each year; (3) at least 75% of total assets must be held in real estate or mortgages; (4) at least 75% of revenues must be from rents on real properties or interest on mortgages secured by real property; (5) there must be a minimum of 100 stockholders, and no five individuals may own 50% or more of the stock.

Net income is not generally used to measure the performance of a REIT, mainly because, for accounting purposes, the value of real estate depreciates regularly over time. Since more often than not market property values rise, the depreciation deduction from net income artificially lowers the reported earnings of REITs. The chief profitability measure is "funds from operations," similar to cash flow. Funds from operations are net income, excluding gains or losses from debt restructuring and sales of property, plus depreciation and amortization. Most REITs report both net income and funds from operations.

The average industry payout ratio (based on funds from operations) is more than 80%. A ratio above 85% to 90% could mean that the dividend may be in jeopardy; a reduction in the payment could be seen if property vacancies increase.

Before you invest in a particular REIT, make sure the operators are experienced in buying and selling properties, as well as in managing them. Management should have an ownership stake of at least 10%. Also, avoid REITs that are highly leveraged. Debt should be no more than 40% of stockholders' equity.

Telephone Companies

At one time, telephone company stocks were tried and true investments for conservative income investors. The companies, notably American Telephone & Telegraph, Continental Telephone, Central Telephone & Utilities, and General Telephone & Electronics, were regulated and could be depended on for steady dividend increases and rising stock prices.

American Telephone & Telegraph was once the largest private company in the world, and "Ma Bell" paid dividends even during the Great Depression. The 1982 settlement of a Justice Department lawsuit against AT&T resulted in the breakup of the company as well as dramatic changes in the telecommunications industry.

AT&T gave up its local telephone operations in exchange for the right to compete in unregulated markets, and it agreed to transfer its holdings in the twenty-two local phone companies to seven regional holding companies of roughly equal assets and revenues. The regionals would not be allowed to provide long-distance service, manufacture telecommunications equipment, or provide information services. (The restriction on information services was lifted in July 1991.)

The environment changed further in 1995 when AT&T decided to split into three separate companies (to provide, respectively, long distance telephone service, equipment manufacturing, and computer technology) and the telecommunications industry was on the verge of being deregulated. Local telephone companies, long-distance carriers, and cable TV operators now are being allowed into each other's markets.

The regional Bell operating companies, with existing lines into homes and businesses, already have a direct link to their customers; but they have never faced the fierce competition of the long-distance market. The long-distance carriers are tough competitors, and, unlike the Bells and the cable operators, have strong national brand names; but they lack direct links to their customers. The cable operators not only have direct links, but also most of their networks are coaxial cable, which has much larger transmission capacity than the copper wire networks commonly used by the regional phone companies. Capacity is critical in providing interactive services, such as games, over these networks, but most cable transmissions are one-way: The customers can't transmit back to the cable company. The regional and long-distance telephone carriers have the essential ability to both transmit to and receive from given locations.

The bottom line is that most of the Bell regionals (Ameritech, Bell Atlantic, BellSouth, SBC Communications and US West), as well as the long distance carriers (AT&T, MCI Communications, and Sprint) are investing in growth opportunities, such as cellular telephones, cable, and international ventures, *and have cut back on dividend increases.* Nevertheless, the stocks as a whole remain attractive for their potential total return (appreciation plus dividends).

Summing Up

1. *Don't buy a stock on the basis of dividend yield alone.*

2. *Make sure the yields of other stocks in the industry are not too far above that of your buy candidate.*

3. *Lean toward lower-yielding stocks with a long history of boosting dividends each year.*

4. *Look at the stock's payout ratio (dividends as a percentage of earnings). Make sure the ratio is not higher than that of the average issue in the industry group.*

5. *Check to see that the company's cash flow is at least three times its dividend payout.*

6. *For a quick check, consult the company's S&P quality ranking.*

3
Nobody Ever Bought Wal-Mart for Its Yield

The biggest threat you face in attempting to meet your financial goals is inflation, the continuing rise in the level of prices paid for goods and services. But why are we even talking about inflation now? Isn't that simply a relic of the early 1980s?

The consumer price index (CPI), the government's official measure of how quickly your money is losing its value, has been fairly stable in recent years. Currently, newspapers are full of stories about the lack of growth in real wages and prices. Companies are cutting staff and increasing their use of technology, always attempting to become more efficient *because they can't raise prices*. Global competition and technological innovation are driving down the cost of many goods and services, especially telecommunications services, computers, semiconductor chips, and other high-tech goods.

Overall the CPI has risen only about 3% annually for several years, a far cry from the 13.3% jump in consumer prices the U.S. experienced during the oil crisis of 1979. Yet even at a low 3% annual increase, the average price of goods and services will still double in twenty-four years. If you're 41 now, that means prices will be twice today's level just when you're ready to retire at age 65. Today's $22,000 car would cost $44,000 in 2020, and that $7.50 movie ticket would be $15. If your child is 17 now, by the time he or she retires at age 65 in 2044, the car would cost $88,000 and the movie ticket would be $30 assuming an inflation rate of only 3% annually.

Of course, 3% inflation is fairly tame by the standards of the last two decades. Let's say inflation averages 4% for the foreseeable future. At that rate, which President Richard Nixon considered so onerous in 1971 that he imposed wage and price controls, prices double every eighteen years. At 6%, less than half the inflation rate at the peak of the last oil crisis, your purchasing power is cut in half in only twelve years. That would mean $15 movie tickets in 2008.

Experts Don't Know, Either

The point is, we don't know if the current inflation rate will persist or if it is simply a dip lasting a few years. You might be tempted to rely on the latest economic forecasts on inflation, but economists can't know the future either. If you don't believe us, save some economic predictions for a year and see how well they age. It doesn't matter if the forecasts are made by the government, private industry, or academic think tanks. Not only will economists disagree with each other, but most will be far off the mark. Consequently, forecasting inflation is little more than making an educated guess. Do you want to base your future on guesswork? You have to be ready to meet your long-term financial goals no matter what the CPI level is in coming years.

Investing in stocks with growing dividends is one of the best ways we know to beat inflation. Table 3-1 clearly shows why. In it, we demonstrate what happens to a hypothetical $10 stock that pays a $0.25 dividend when that dividend grows by 10% a year and the share price increases by the same percentage. At the end of 10 years, your current yield remains 2.5% of the most recent share price. But for long-term investors, the best way to value your dividend is to view it as a yield on your original investment. After all, though the *value* of your investment has risen over the years, *your cost has not changed.* The stock you bought for $10 is now worth $23.57, but you still paid $10 for it. And now you are getting a $0.59 annual dividend, which means that the yield on your cost is 5.9%.

A yield of 5.9% may not seem like much when you look at the recent returns of some stocks that don't pay dividends. But remember, as long as the dividend isn't cut, your annual yield on your original investment will never fall below 5.9%. In fact, if the company has a strong

Table 3-1. Effects of an Increasing Dividend

Year	Stock Price $	Dividend $	Current Yield %	Yield on Cost %
1	10.00	0.25	2.5	2.5
2	11.00	0.28	2.5	2.8
3	12.10	0.30	2.5	3.0
4	13.31	0.33	2.5	3.3
5	14.64	0.37	2.5	3.7
6	16.11	0.40	2.5	4.0
7	17.72	0.44	2.5	4.4
8	19.49	0.49	2.5	4.9
9	21.43	0.54	2.5	5.4
10	23.57	0.59	2.5	5.9

history of dividend increases, it is likely to go higher. And 5.9% is more than half the average annual total return of stocks (as measured by the S&P 500 index) since 1928.

Beyond Hypothetical

Let's look at a real-world example of dividend growth. Suppose you bought 100 shares of Wal-Mart, the discount retailer, in 1973. Since the price of a stock fluctuates, let's also assume you paid the average of the high and low prices that Wal-Mart traded at during 1973. That would make your cost per share 23⅝ or $2,362.50 (excluding brokerage commission) for your "round lot" of 100 shares. At the time, Wal-Mart had been public for only a few years and was considered a fast-growing regional retailer. In 1973, the company paid its first dividend of $0.05 a share, which would have provided you with $5 on your 100 shares, or a yield of 0.2% ($5/$2,362.50) on your investment. Clearly, that yield was nothing to get excited about.

Jump ahead to 1995. Wal-Mart is the world's largest retailer with more than 2,400 stores and warehouse clubs in the United States, Canada, Mexico, Brazil, Argentina, and Hong Kong. The stock's annual dividend per share in 1995 was only $0.20, for a yield of about 0.8% on its average share price of 24. Again, a yield that few would consider generous.

But we've left out a few details about Wal-Mart's rise over the twenty-two years since it paid its first dividend. The company increased its dividend every year and split its shares frequently. In fact, there were eight 2-for-1 stock splits in Wal-Mart shares over those twenty-two years. The splits turned the 100 shares you would have purchased in 1973 into 25,600 shares by 1995. Each of those shares paid a $0.20 annual dividend, resulting in a total dividend payment of $5,120 in 1995. That's a dividend increase of 102,300% in twenty-two years. Put another way, your current dividend as a yield on your original investment is 217% ($5,120/ $2,362.50). Now *that's* a yield to get excited about. And we haven't even mentioned that your initial investment of less than $2,400 has grown to be worth about $600,000.

By now, you're probably thinking that Wal-Mart was a great buy in 1973. But who knew? Who *could* have known? In fact, you're right. Very few people had the foresight to buy Wal-Mart stock in 1973 and stick with it for more than 20 years.

Yet, what if you had purchased the shares 10 years ago? At an average price of 53⅜, 100 shares of Wal-Mart would have cost $5,337.50 in 1985. The stock paid $0.28 a share in dividends for a yield of 0.5%. By 1995, you would have owned 1,600 shares (after splits) worth about $38,000 and yielding an annual 6% on your original investment.

Admittedly, a 6% annual yield is not 217%, but it is more than twice the recent inflation rate and far more than double the recent yield on stocks in general. What might have led you to Wal-Mart stock a decade ago? For one thing, a solid record. By then, Wal-Mart had given its shareholders more than a decade of dividend increases. Although there are no guarantees, companies that regularly increase dividends are a good bet to continue doing so and are ideal for long-term investors. As legendary portfolio manager Peter Lynch notes in his book, *Beating the Street*,* "The dividend is such an important factor in the success of many stocks that you could hardly go wrong by making an entire portfolio of companies that have raised their dividends for 10 or 20 years in a row."

Table 3-2 lists 105 companies that have increased their dividends every year for the ten years through 1995. To weed out companies that make only nominal yearly dividend increases, we screened out companies with ten-year cumulative dividend growth under 200%. That gave us a comfortable edge on inflation, which in the last decade has seen prices rise about 50%. Finally, we wanted a significant current yield on the average price of the shares 10 years ago. Each of the stocks in the table yields at least 6% on that assumed "cost" of the shares.

*Lynch, Peter with John Rothchild (1993) *Beating the Street*. New York: Simon & Schuster.

Table 3-2. Stocks with Good Yields on Cost

Company	Ticker	S&P Rank	1985 Average Price	1995 Indicated Div.	% Yield on 1985 Average Price	10-year Div. Increase (%)
AFLAC Inc.	AFL	A	$6.97	$0.52	7.5	272.5
Abbott Laboratories	ABT	A+	6.99	0.84	12.0	397.9
Air Products & Chemicals	APD	A	14.09	1.04	7.4	227.6
Albertson's Inc.	ABS	A+	3.72	0.52	14.0	462.2
Alfa Corp.	ALFA	A	2.84	0.38	13.4	270.7
ALLIED Group	ALGR	A	8.83	0.68	7.7	1175.8
Anheuser-Busch Cos.	BUD	A+	17.34	1.76	10.2	380.2
Associated Banc-Corp.	ASBC	A+	9.04	1.08	11.9	333.4
AVEMCO Corp.	AVE	B+	6.30	0.48	7.6	260.1
Avery Dennison Corp.	AVY	B+	17.34	1.20	6.9	287.1
Baldor Electric	BEZ	A	5.42	0.36	6.7	305.4
Banc One Corp.	ONE	A+	11.05	1.36	12.3	273.4
BancorpSouth	BOMS	A	6.39	0.68	10.7	229.3
Bard (C.R.)	BCR	A–	8.20	0.64	7.8	412.0
Baxter International	BAX	B+	14.62	1.13	7.7	213.9

Table 3-2. Stocks with Good Yields on Cost *(cont'd)*

Company	Ticker	S&P Rank	1985 Average Price	1995 Indicated Div.	% Yield on 1985 Average Price	10-year Div. Increase (%)
Bemis Co.	BMS	A	$4.38	$0.64	14.6	412.0
Block (H & R)	HRB	A	7.71	1.28	16.6	312.9
Brady(W.H.) Cl "A"	BRCOA	A–	17.19	1.20	7.0	1101.2
Bristol-Myers Squibb	BMY	A+	29.38	3.00	10.2	231.5
Brown-Forman Cl "B"	BF.B	A	8.73	1.04	11.9	398.1
Campbell Soup	CPB	B	11.04	1.38	12.5	341.6
Central Fidelity Banks	CFBS	A	11.13	1.20	10.8	240.5
Cincinnati Financial	CINF	A	15.22	1.36	8.9	273.3
Clorox Co.	CLX	A	19.50	2.12	10.9	221.2
Coca-Cola Co.	KO	A+	6.15	0.88	14.3	256.9
Comerica Inc.	CMA	A–	8.83	1.40	15.9	200.0
Compass Bancshares	CBSS	A	8.11	1.12	13.8	242.9
ConAgra Inc.	CAG	A+	8.13	0.95	11.7	373.8
Cooper Tire & Rubber	CTB	A	2.19	0.30	13.7	500.0

Company	Symbol	Rating				
CORUS Bankshares	CORS	A	3.69	0.40	10.8	1233.3
Crawford & Co. Cl "B"	CRD.B	A	5.22	0.54	10.3	237.5
Disney (Walt) Co.	DIS	A	5.52	0.36	6.5	380.0
Eaton Vance	EV	A–	7.88	0.68	8.6	518.2
Electronic Data Systems	EDS	A+	8.38	0.52	6.2	967.8
Ennis Business Forms	EBF	A	5.63	0.60	10.7	532.9
Federal National Mortgage	FNM	A–	7.26	2.72	37.4	5003.2
Fifth Third Bancorp	FITB	A+	10.23	1.56	15.2	404.3
First Empire State	FES	A+	28.94	2.80	9.7	348.0
First Michigan Bank	FMBC	A+	5.18	0.84	16.2	344.7
First Northern Capital	FNGB	B+	6.25	0.56	9.0	282.3
First Union Corp.	FTU	A	19.96	2.08	10.4	261.7
Firstar Corp.	FSR	B+	9.06	1.36	15.0	325.9
Flowers Industries	FLO	B+	8.86	0.57	6.5	200.1

Table 3-2. Stocks with Good Yields on Cost *(cont'd)*

Company	Ticker	S&P Rank	1985 Average Price	1995 Indicated Div.	% Yield on 1985 Average Price	10-year Div. Increase (%)
Franklin Resources	BEN	A	$3.41	$0.44	12.9	2650.0
Gillette Co.	G	A+	3.91	0.60	15.3	269.2
Glacier Bancorp	GBCI	A+	2.67	0.64	24.0	732.2
Hach Co.	HACH	A	3.23	0.24	7.4	633.9
Hannaford Bros.	HRD	A+	5.29	0.42	7.9	252.9
Harland (John H.)	JH	A	15.62	1.02	6.5	264.3
Hartford Steam Boiler	HSB	B+	11.59	2.28	19.7	444.5
Health Care Property Investors	HCP	NR	10.63	2.20	20.7	502.7
Heinz (H.J.)	HNZ	A+	9.13	1.06	11.6	285.5
Hillenbrand Industries	HB	A	5.81	0.60	10.3	344.4
Hormel Foods	HRL	A+	5.19	0.60	11.6	344.4
Hubbell Inc. Cl "B"	HUB.B	A	17.26	1.88	10.9	233.3
Huntington Bancshares	HBAN	A−	6.09	0.80	13.1	267.3

Illinois Tool Works	ITW	A+	7.94	0.68	8.6	300.0
International Flavors & Fragrences	IFF	A+	11.00	1.36	12.4	264.3
Interpublic Group	IPG	A+	6.41	0.62	9.7	244.4
Johnson & Johnson	JNJ	A+	11.29	1.32	11.7	314.2
Kellogg Co.	K	A+	13.81	1.56	11.3	246.7
KeyCorp	KEY	A+	11.27	1.44	12.8	213.0
Keystone Financial	KSTN	A–	13.06	1.44	11.0	260.0
Kimberly-Clark	KMB	A+	14.38	1.80	12.5	214.4
Lilly (Eli)	LLY	A	11.01	1.37	12.4	242.5
Loctite Corp.	LOC	A	8.00	1.00	12.5	400.0
Mark Twain Bancshares	MTWN	A	10.11	1.08	10.7	203.8
Medtronic Inc.	MDT	A+	2.17	0.26	12.0	433.9
Mercantile Bankshares	MRBK	A	9.72	0.92	9.5	217.2
Merck & Co.	MRK	A+	6.33	1.36	21.5	665.3
Modine Manufacturing	MODI	A	4.68	0.60	12.8	269.2

Table 3-2. Stocks with Good Yields on Cost *(cont'd)*

Company	Ticker	S&P Rank	1985 Average Price	1995 Indicated Div.	% Yield on 1985 Average Price	10-year Div. Increase (%)
National Penn Bancshares	NPBC	NR	$8.11	$0.88	10.9	413.7
NationsBank Corp.	NB	A–	20.24	2.32	11.5	238.7
Northern Trust	NTRS	B+	8.04	1.24	15.4	310.3
PepsiCo Inc.	PEP	A+	6.44	0.80	12.4	449.8
Philip Morris Cos.	MO	A+	10.45	4.00	38.3	731.3
Pitney Bowes	PBI	A+	10.43	1.20	11.5	300.0
Premier Industrial	PRE	A	7.14	0.50	7.0	369.0
Raymond James Financial	RJF	A–	2.39	0.38	15.9	1457.4
Reuters Holdings ADS	RTRSY	NR	6.57	0.85	12.9	1193.8
Rubbermaid Inc.	RBD	A	7.09	0.56	7.9	397.8
Schering-Plough	SGP	A+	6.36	1.16	18.3	452.4
Sonoco Products	SON	A–	6.09	0.60	9.8	250.1
SouthTrust Corp.	SOTR	A	6.95	0.80	11.5	221.7
Stanhome Inc.	STH	A–	6.00	1.06	17.7	253.3
State Street Boston	STT	A+	8.05	0.72	8.9	409.9
Student Loan Marketing	SLM	A	12.65	1.60	12.6	2122.2

Company	Ticker	Rating				
SunTrust Banks	STI	A+	17.75	1.60	9.0	433.3
Synovus Financial	SNV	A+	6.86	0.54	7.9	352.3
Sysco Corp.	SYY	A+	4.88	0.52	10.7	940.0
Temple-Inland	TIN	B+	15.25	1.20	7.9	368.7
Torchmark Corp.	TMK	A+	13.79	1.16	8.4	231.4
UST Inc.	UST	A+	4.33	1.48	34.2	588.4
United Fire & Casualty	UFCS	B+	7.25	0.90	12.4	238.7
U.S. Bancorp	USBC	A	8.65	1.12	12.9	262.9
Universal Foods	UFC	A	7.94	1.00	12.6	212.5
Valspar Corp.	VAL	A+	6.20	0.66	10.6	500.0
Wachovia Corp.	WB	A−	10.41	1.44	13.8	252.7
Wal-Mart Stores	WMT	A+	3.33	0.20	6.0	1119.5
Walgreen Co.	WAG	A+	6.46	0.44	6.8	287.0
Warner-Lambert	WLA	A−	20.68	2.60	12.6	246.7
Washington Federal	WFSL	A	4.33	0.96	22.2	799.7
Wausau Paper Mills	WSAU	A−	2.04	0.28	13.7	451.2
Wilmington Trust Corp.	WILM	A+	7.50	1.20	16.0	336.4
York Financial	YFED	B+	3.76	0.54	14.3	459.7
S&P 500			**187.85**	**14.19**	**7.6**	**80.0**

In fact, many of these stocks now provide double-digit yields on their 10-year-ago prices. Assuming there are no dividend cuts, that means owners of these stocks who have held them for a decade will outpace the average total return that the stock market has posted for more than sixty years *with just the dividends from these issues.* Again, we have not even considered the price appreciation of these stocks over the decade.

Why do these companies make regular, substantial increases in their dividends? One reason is simply that they can. Take a close look at the stocks in the table. Many are familiar names from the traditional "growth stock" universe, including Coca-Cola, Gillette, and Walt Disney Co. These are companies that consistently increase earnings. So why bother looking at dividends? Why not simply look at earnings growth to pick stocks?

Earnings growth alone can be misleading. A charge against earnings, perhaps because of an acquisition, can distort the year-to-year growth picture. What's more, owning high-growth stocks that don't pay dividends exposes your portfolio to greater volatility (as we explained in Chap. 1) and can deprive you of any returns in a bear market.

Another reason that companies pay increasing dividends is to create investor loyalty. As we have noted, a stock is less likely to be dumped by an individual who is looking forward to the next quarterly payment. And when that payment represents a double-digit return on the original investment, the incentive to hold is even greater. That helps to put a floor under the price of the stock.

When company managers own shares or receive part of their compensation in options on shares, keeping that stock price from "tanking" during a brief period of market or industry uncertainty becomes an important goal.

Does that mean that every stock in our list of 105 companies will raise its dividend annually for the next ten years? Of course not. In investing there are no guarantees. Consider Deluxe Corporation, a company that would have made our list until directors voted in August 1995 to keep the quarterly dividend at $0.37. Prior to that action, Deluxe, a major check printer and supplier of computer forms and financial software, had increased its dividend for 34 consecutive years.

The move by Deluxe to hold its dividend steady doesn't mean that it's a bad company or that its stock is a poor investment. In fact, with some weakness in the company's businesses and an uneven earnings growth record in recent years, Deluxe directors probably made a prudent move in conserving resources by not raising the dividend. But if you are looking to increase your investment returns by selecting companies with rising dividends, there are better candidates listed in Table 3-2.

Take a close look at that list. You may be surprised to find not a single electric utility among the stocks. (Baldor Electric may sound like a power company, but it isn't. The company makes electric motors.) Although many utilities increase their dividends annually, those increases seldom outpace inflation. Utilities generally have higher *current* yields and are attractive if you need income now. But if you are planning to retire ten years or more into the future, your retirement income stream will be higher if you pick stocks that rapidly increase their dividends.

The industry group that dominates our list is financial services, with banks, insurers, and mutual fund management companies accounting for about 40% of all the stocks listed. In particular, regional banks stand out. Perhaps they increased dividends substantially because past restrictions on interstate banking prevented them from using profits to buy banks in neighboring states. As the banking industry consolidates, some of these companies will not survive as independents. But that should not stop you from investing in them, since it is likely that many will be acquired by even larger banks at a premium price.

Food and beverage companies constitute a bit more than 10% of our list. Among the household names in this group are Campbell Soup, H.J. Heinz, Kellogg, and PepsiCo. Their branded prepared food products command higher profit margins than ingredients in meals that must be made from scratch. When those high profit margins are made on millions of sales driven by thousands of advertising messages, significant earnings power results. Those earnings are, in part, returned to investors via steadily rising dividends.

Drug and medical supply companies also make up roughly 10% of our list. Well-known names in this group include Abbott Laboratories, Bristol-Myers Squibb, Johnson & Johnson, and Merck. Because of patent protection on their pharmaceuticals and medical devices, these companies, too, enjoy high profit margins. Increasing dividends are the investors' reward.

The list also includes supermarket chains (Albertson's, Hannaford Bros.), forest products companies (Temple-Inland, Wausau Paper Mills), specialty chemicals producers (Air Products & Chemicals, Valspar Corp.) and tobacco companies (Philip Morris Cos., UST). Not all will do in the next ten years what they did in the last ten. Your best approach is to investigate the companies carefully before you invest in their stocks and to diversify across industries.

Summing Up

1. *You can't meet your financial goals if you don't beat inflation.*

2. *With inflation at a "low" 3% annually, prices will double every twenty-four years.*

3. *Buying stocks of companies that regularly and substantially increase their dividends is an excellent way to outpace inflation.*

4. *You should view a stock's current dividend as a yield on what you paid for the stock (your "cost basis"). Although the dividend rose, your cost didn't.*

5. *Stocks with dividends that grow into a double-digit yield on your cost outperform the historical total return of the stock market with their dividends alone.*

6. *Although most companies that have increased their dividends regularly for a decade will continue to do so, some won't.*

7. *Make sure your portfolio is diversified across several industries to avoid putting all your eggs in one basket.*

"Free"4 Stocks

The elderly widow had come to this country from Europe a half-century earlier. She and her late husband had worked hard, raised a family, and saved what they could. Over the years, she had become comfortably middle class, not rich. Certainly she would never have considered herself an "investor." Only rich people could afford to invest; she saved. Yet at some point she had bought a few shares of a gas utility and held the stock—the only one she ever owned—for the rest of her life.

In her later years, she looked forward to the dividend check that arrived like clockwork every quarter. Clearly it pleased her to have a small sum of money materialize in the mailbox four times a year. Her grandson noticed her reaction to the dividend checks and it puzzled him. A preadolescent, he was just beginning to understand how money really works. He knew the dividend checks were not his grandmother's total means of support and that the shares they represented were worth considerably more than the quarterly payments.

"Why do you keep that stock?" he asked his grandmother one day when the check arrived. "The check is only a few dollars. Wouldn't you be better off selling the shares and putting the money in the bank?"

"You don't understand, child," she answered. "Over the years, these checks have paid me back for the stock."

The story is true and the grandchild always remembered the lesson. Unfortunately, it's a lesson that few investors recognize today. And investment professionals are likely to dismiss it for two reasons, both of which make sense, and neither of which should really matter to you.

Time and Taxes

The first objection to the idea that dividends pay back your investment has to do with a concept called the "time value of money." Basically, money you have today is worth more than money you will have tomorrow. As we saw in Chap. 3, inflation eats away at the value of money, even funds that you invest. The $100 in your pocket today can be invested and earn a return, making it worth more than the $100 you get next year. The second objection is that taxes cut into the real return that dividends provide, making it take much longer for a true payback of your investment.

Essentially, both objections to the concept that dividends pay you back for the cost of your shares quibble over time. Consider a hypothetical stock that never fluctuates in price and provides a consistent 10% yield. Without taking into account the effects of inflation and taxes, this stock would pay back its cost in ten years. But an owner of the stock who is in the 28% tax bracket would receive an after-tax yield of only 7.2%. Allowing for taxes, the stock would pay back its cost in dividends in a little less than fourteen years. Similar adjustments can be made for the effects of inflation.

Maintaining Ownership

The point is not how long it takes to return your entire investment. If you are a long-term holder of a stock with a substantial or growing dividend, the point is that the cost of your investment can be returned *while you still own it.* That means you will still participate in the stock's future appreciation and dividend growth even though you have recaptured your entire original investment.

As we noted in Chap. 1, unless you want to get involved with options, the only way to realize a return on a stock that does not pay a dividend is to sell that stock. Once you sell the stock, you have created what the folks at the Internal Revenue Service call a "taxable event." Even if it's at a lower capital gains tax rate, you will have to pay taxes on your gain all at once. In contrast, the dividend-paying stock spreads out your return—and the taxes on it—over time.

Table 4-1 lists a group of stocks that paid for themselves in dividends over a decade. As the "cost" of each stock, we used the average of the high and low prices in 1985. We then added up the stream of dividends for the ten years from 1986 through 1995. Since the final year of our test was not yet over when we created this list, we used the indicated dividend as of early December 1995.

Our list eliminates stocks that sold for less than $5 (adjusted for splits) in 1985. We also left out companies that made large extra dividend payments to shareholders over the course of the decade. These were often one-time payments due to restructurings, such as the sale of a division, and don't really represent regular dividends. Even so, removing extra-dividend payers caused us to drop one interesting company from the list. Wm. Wrigley, the world's leading maker of chewing gum, has for many years paid its shareholders a substantial *annual* extra dividend. In mid-December 1995, Wrigley paid its holders an additional $0.37 a share. That's quite a bonus considering the company's indicated dividend at the time was $0.68. Even though it didn't make the list, Wrigley has been a superb investment with a 29% average annual total return over the ten years ended 1995. The company has paid a dividend since 1913. With 50% of the U.S. chewing gum market and a presence in the growing markets of Eastern Europe, China, and India, Wrigley should continue to provide investors with solid returns.

Table 4-1. "Free" Stocks

Company	Ticker	Rank	Total Per-share Dividend Paid over 10 Years	Average Price 10 Years Ago
AGL Resources	ATG	B+	$9.5600	$8.25
Allegheny Power System	AYP	A–	15.6500	15.62
ALLTEL Corp.	AT	A	6.6903	6.00
Amer Bank of Conn.	BKC	B+	11.9700	11.13
American Electric Power	AEP	B+	23.7000	22.37
Ameritech Corp.	AIT	A–	16.0200	15.08
Bangor Hydro Electric	BGR	B+	11.5400	8.74
Bay State Gas	BGC	A–	12.5113	10.83
Bell Atlantic Corp.	BEL	A–	23.4050	23.13
Berkshire Gas	BGAS	B1	1.6000	11.25
Bradley Real Estate	BTR	NR	12.9372	12.04
Capstead Mortgage	CMO	NR	17.1998	13.41
Carolina Power & Light	CPL	A–	15.1800	13.75
Central & South West	CSR	A–	14.1500	12.44
Central Maine Power	CTP	B	13.8400	11.81
Central VT Public Service	CV	B	12.9530	12.88
Cincinnati Bell	CSN	B+	6.8500	6.17
CINergy Corp.	CIN	B	15.9342	12.04
Colonial Gas	CGES	B+	11.7345	11.29
Commonwealth Energy Sys.	CES	B+	28.6100	26.56
Connecticut Energy	CNE	A–	12.2325	12.00
Consolidated Edison	ED	A	17.7000	17.24
DPL, Inc.	DPL	B+	10.4996	7.96
Detroit Edison	DTE	B+	18.4450	15.94
Dominion Resources	D	A–	22.6895	21.20
Duke Power	DUK	A–	16.4500	16.34
Enova Corp.	ENA	A–	13.7000	12.50

Table 4-1. "Free" Stocks *(cont'd)*

Company	Ticker	Rank	Total Per-share Dividend Paid over 10 Years	Average Price 10 Years Ago
ESELCO, Inc.	EDSE	A–	$8.5954	$7.45
Empire District Electric	EDE	A–	11.6545	10.78
Essex County Gas	ECGC	A	13.5100	12.37
Federal National Mortgage	FNM	A–	10.9566	7.26
First Hawaiian	FHWN	A	8.5100	7.50
Ford Motor	F	B–	10.2065	8.27
GTE Corp.	GTE	B+	15.3650	14.07
General Public Utilities	GPU	B	11.4600	6.99
Green Mountain Power	GMP	A–	19.3900	17.75
Hartford Steam Boiler Insurance	HSB	B+	16.2100	11.59
Health Care Prop. Inv.	HCP	NR	15.9390	10.63
Health Care REIT	HCN	NR	17.8650	14.77
Houston Industries	HOU	B+	29.4200	25.63
IES Industries	IES	B+	20.5300	19.63
Indiana Energy	IEI	B+	8.8797	8.62
Interlake Corp	IK	NR	49.9000	24.34
IPALCO Enterprises	IPL	B+	18.4900	17.84
KU Energy	KU	A	14.7300	13.81
Kansas City Power & Light	KLT	B+	13.1350	10.63
Long Island Lighting	LIL	B	9.9450	7.56
Lukens, Inc.	LUC	B+	7.6336	6.05
Madison Gas & Electric	MDSN	A–	17.3092	16.62
Maine Public Service	MAP	B	14.1950	8.05
Meditrust	MT	NR	22.2608	12.50
Merck & Co.	MRK	A+	7.1920	6.33

Company	Ticker	Rank	Total Per-share Dividend Paid over 10 Years	Average Price 10 Years Ago
Merry Land & Investment	MRY	NR	$6.9500	$5.44
Minnesota Power & Light	MPL	B+	18.4200	17.50
Montana Power	MTP	B+	14.5000	13.28
Nationwide Health Prop.	NHP	NR	21.0325	18.94
Nevada Power	NVP	B+	15.5100	15.18
New Jersey Resources	NJR	B+	13.9900	13.43
New Plan Realty Trust	NPR	NR	10.9050	10.54
North Carolina Natural Gas	NCG	A−	9.1262	7.77
Northeast Utilities	NU	B	17.5200	16.25
Northwestern Public Service	NPS	A	14.7925	11.34
NYNEX Corp.	NYN	B+	21.6100	21.41
Oklahoma Gas & Electric	OGE	A−	24.6200	24.56
Otter Tail Power	OTTR	A−	15.8400	15.62
PECO Energy	PE	B	17.4250	15.75
PP&L Resources	PPL	A−	14.9725	13.13
Pacific Telesis Group	PAC	B+	19.4925	19.05
Pennsylvania REIT	PEI	NR	16.8199	15.72
Philip Morris Cos.	MO	A+	17.8834	10.45
Piedmont Natural Gas	PNY	A−	8.4300	8.29
Pittsburgh & W. Va. RR	PW	NR	5.5250	5.50
Potomac Electric Power	POM	B+	14.9600	14.78
Public Service Enterprise Group	PEG	B+	20.8660	19.49
Puget Sound Power & Light	PSD	B+	17.8600	15.50
SBC Communications	SBC	A	13.6040	13.07
St. Joseph Light & Power	SAJ	A−	15.8233	14.16
SCANA Corp.	SCG	A−	12.7500	12.56

Table 4-1. "Free" Stocks *(cont'd)*

Company	Ticker	Rank	Total Per-share Dividend Paid over 10 Years	Average Price 10 Years Ago
Southeastern Michigan Gas Ent.	SMGS	A	$6.2898	$5.41
Southern California Water	SCW	B+	10.8600	10.50
Southern Co.	SO	A–	11.0225	10.40
Southern Indiana Gas & Electric	SIG	A	14.3593	14.02
Stanhome, Inc.	STH	A–	7.7950	6.00
TECO Energy	TE	A	8.2625	8.05
UGI Corp.	UGI	B+	11.8850	11.03
Union Electric	UEP	A–	21.4650	18.62
United Dominion Realty Trust	UDR	NR	6.3450	6.31
United Illuminating	UIL	B	24.7150	20.44
UNITIL Corp.	UTL	B+	10.2618	8.38
Upper Peninsula Energy	UPEN	B+	11.2890	10.06
UtiliCorp United	UCU	A–	13.8690	13.45
Valley Resources	VR	A–	5.9247	5.06
WPL Holdings	WPH	A	17.4500	17.41
Weingarten Realty	WRI	NR	19.2800	12.61
Wells Fargo	WFC	B+	28.9200	27.63

Utilities Dominate

Of the 95 companies on our list, utilities (electric, gas, and water companies) constitute the largest segment, at 69%. Real estate investment trusts (REITs) are next, at 13%. Why do these groups dominate this list when they don't even appear in Table 3-1, which shows stocks that have increased their dividends annually and now yield at least 6% on their 10-year-ago prices? The reason is quite simple. In the screen of stocks that we did for the last chapter, we were looking for companies that increased their dividends substantially over a decade. A requirement for inclusion in Table 3-1 was that a company grew its dividend by at least 200% over the course of the decade. While many utilities and REITs increase their dividends annually, they usually can't raise their payments that rapidly. On average, utilities and REITs already sport large payout ratios (dividends as a percent of earnings)—80% or more in the case of many electric utilities and 95% (by law!) for a company to qualify as a REIT. Stocks with high payout ratios can't increase dividends 200% in a decade because their earnings simply don't grow that fast. As a result, most of the stocks on this list are better suited to people who need current income rather than to those planning for retirement in a decade or more. In Chap. 9, we'll offer some suggestions and sample portfolios for individuals who need to live on their investment income.

Financial services companies, which dominated our list in Chap. 3, account for only 6% of the stocks in Table 4-1. Three financial services companies, Federal National Mortgage, Hartford Steam Boiler Inspection and Insurance, and Washington Federal, appear on both lists and are worth considering as long-term investments.

Federal National Mortgage, better known in the market as "Fannie Mae," is a government-sponsored, publicly traded company that packages home mortgages as securities. In plain language, Fannie Mae buys loans from mortgage originators, bundles together those with similar characteristics, and sells these mortgage-backed securities to investors. One of the main reasons that mortgages are so easily obtainable in the U.S. is that Fannie Mae and similar organizations enable lenders to convert long-term mortgages into fresh cash that then becomes available again to home buyers in the form of new mortgages. On the other side of the equation, Fannie Mae insures the loans it packages and resells to investors against default. When investors can buy securities backed by mortgages without fear that a homeowner in a distant town may default, they are more willing to lend. That willingness is what makes the mortgage market in this country work.

Fannie Mae's success is reflected in its stock. In the five years ended 1995, the stock produced an average annual total return of 32%. Earnings have risen dramatically, and dividends have grown more than 5,000% in the last decade. The stock split 3-for-1 in 1989 and 4-for-1 in February 1996. Since our table was created late in 1995, it does not reflect the 1996 split.

Hartford Steam Boiler is a specialty insurance and engineering services company. Founded in 1866 to insure boilers, the company now provides commercial loss coverage for other specialty items, including air conditioning and computer systems. Unlike most insurers, HSB has its own engineers inspect machinery to be insured in an attempt to control losses. Although HSB has been a stellar performer for many years, the stock's total return dropped to only 5.1% annually over the last five years. More difficult conditions in the property-casualty insurance business caused earnings to decline in both 1992 and 1993. Despite the earnings weakness, HSB's directors expressed their confidence in the future by continuing to increase the dividend. From 1991 through 1995, the company's dividend rose 23%. Hartford Steam Boiler has increased its international business and tightened its underwriting standard to improve profitability. In 1995, the stock rebounded with a total return of 31% for the year. With a secure dividend providing a 4.5% yield (at year-end 1995), the stock looks attractive for long-term total return.

Washington Federal is a $4.6 billion Seattle-based savings and loan with eighty-nine branches in Washington, Idaho, Oregon, Utah, and Arizona. Founded in 1917, WFSL is a traditional S&L with more than 75% of its loan receivables in single-family residential mortgages. Because the company specializes in 30-year fixed-rate loans, it is exposed to interest rate risk. When the Federal Reserve Board increases short-term interest rates, as it did in late 1994 and early 1995, WFSL's earnings are squeezed. Despite the uncertainties of the market in which it operates, Washington Federal's dividend growth has been spectacular. Over the last decade, dividends have increased almost 800%. The stock's average annual total return for the five years through 1995 was 13.9%.

Eight percent of the stocks that paid for themselves in dividends over the decade studied are phone companies. Traditionally, phone companies have been excellent investments for the long-term, conservative investor. While we still expect shares of providers of local telephone service to sport higher-than-average yields, increasing competition from cable companies, long distance services, and newer technologies will slow the growth of dividends at phone companies. They are still worth having in your portfolio, but not necessarily as stocks for current income. Among those phone companies in our list, we believe that ALLTEL Corp., Ameritech, Bell Atlantic, and SBC Communications are well positioned to post strong returns under deregulation.

Five stocks in Table 4-1 came from none of the above groups. Ford Motor made the list primarily because its stock was depressed a decade ago. As a cyclical company (one whose fortunes are closely tied to the economy's cycles of expansion and contraction), Ford has had an erratic earnings and dividend pattern. Investing in auto stocks requires close attention to the cycles of the business, and we don't recommend the group for long-term total return. Another cyclical issue that appears on the list is Lukens, a steel maker. Its stock, too, was depressed in 1985, a year in which the company posted a loss due to non-recurring charges. Despite widely fluctuating earnings, Lukens has paid fairly steady and slowly-growing dividends for the last decade. Nevertheless, the cyclical nature of the steel business makes this stock less suitable for conservative total-return investors.

Merck & Co. is the only pharmaceutical stock to show up both in our strong dividend growth table in Chap. 3 and in this chapter's table of stocks that paid for themselves in dividends. One of our all-time favorites, the stock had a five-year average annual total return of 20.5% and should continue to post strong earnings and dividend gains in the coming years. Ditto for Philip Morris, which also shows up on both lists. The key worry here is that tobacco liability suits and further restrictions on cigarette smoking could cause the stock price to tumble. Stanhome, a marketer of giftware, collectibles, and home care and personal care items, is on both lists, too. Although earnings in recent years have been somewhat erratic, they should improve based on recent efforts to cut direct marketing costs. Dividends have grown steadily, and the company has no long-term debt.

Lower Yields Now

With 1995's market surge and a general slowdown in corporate dividend increases, it will be harder for most stocks to pay for themselves in dividends over the coming decade. Consider that typical yields on utilities fell some 37% over the last decade, from 7.3% at the end of 1985 to 4.6% in late 1995. Right now, dividend growth has slowed, in part because strong market advances keep shareholders happy. They see the prices of their stocks rising steadily and tend not to care much about dividends. Also, companies recently have been buying back their stock with funds that would normally go to increasing dividends. When a company repurchases its stock, per-share earnings and per-share book value (assets minus liabilities) rise because there are fewer shares outstanding. That, in turn, boosts the price of the stock. The price rises also because the buyback increases demand and decreases supply.

When the market once again heads south or trades in a narrow range for a long period of time, however, shareholders will demand a greater current return on their investments. That's when you can expect more frequent increases in dividends from a large number of companies.

History supports this theory. Over the past four decades, dividend increases on common stocks have averaged 1,676 a year. Yet in the period 1973 through 1982, which included the worst bear market in recent memory, companies averaged 2,395 dividend increases a year—almost 43% more increases. The bull market decades immediately before and after the bear market saw average annual dividend increases of 1,563 and 1,531, respectively.

Summing Up

1. *Despite the effects of inflation and taxes, stocks with secure high dividends or steadily growing dividends will pay back their cost if held for the long term.*

2. *Traditional high-yield stocks, such as utilities and REITs, are good choices if you need current income.*

3. *Companies that have grown dividends rapidly and have paid back their cost in dividends over the last decade are particularly good choices for long-term total return. These include Federal National Mortgage (Fannie Mae), Hartford Steam Boiler, Merck, Philip Morris, Stanhome, and Washington Federal.*

4. *Because of increased competition, phone companies are not likely to increase their dividends as quickly in the decade ahead. Nevertheless, we still like ALLTEL Corp., Ameritech, Bell Atlantic, and SBC Communications for growth and income in the coming years.*

5. *Slower dividend growth means that it will take longer for stocks to pay back their cost in coming years. History suggests that dividend growth should accelerate when the market advance stalls for an extended period of time.*

5
Increasing the Power of Dividends

The word "compounding" is rarely used alone in financial publications. It's preceded by either "power" or "magic," as in the power of compounding or the magic of compounding. The added nouns are not hyperbole. Compounding, which is the way your investment grows as it earns returns on your initial money invested and on the interest or dividends earned, can be truly amazing. An investment of only $100 a year earning 8% will grow to $7,311 in twenty-five years, compounded annually. You will have invested only $2,500 in that time, but your earnings will total $4,811. That's an average annual return of 23.4%. If you invested $100 annually at a 10% rate, it would be worth close to $10,000 in twenty-five years, for an average return of more than 39% a year.

To find out quickly how long it would take to double your money at different rates, use the Rule of 72. Simply divide 72 by the yield. If you earn 6%, for example, it will take twelve years to double your money (72/6=12); at 7%, it will take ten years; at 8%, nine years, and so on.

To find out how long it takes to triple your money, use the Rule of 115. Divide the rate of return into 115. For example, an investment earning an 8% return will triple in 14 years. See Table 5-1 for the way the Rule of 72 works using a $1,000 investment returning 8% annually.

Reinvesting Dividends

Let's take a look at how reinvesting dividends can work its magic. The S&P 500 index, which is regarded by professional money managers as a proxy for the general market, climbed 353% over the fifteen years that ended in

Table 5-1. Compounding the "Rule of 72"

Year	Starting $ Amount	Earnings	Ending $ Amount
1	1,000	80	1,080
2	1,080	86	1,166
3	1,166	93	1,259
4	1,259	101	1,360
5	1,360	109	1,469
6	1,469	117	1,586
7	1,586	127	1,713
8	1,713	137	1,850
9	1,850	148	1,998

1995. Not too shabby. But if you plowed back the dividends, the gain nearly doubled to 694%. Put another way, if you had invested $1,000 fifteen years ago in the S&P 500 index, you'd now have $4,530. With dividends reinvested, though, that total balloons to $7,940. Over the ten years ended 1995, the S&P 500, with reinvested dividends, gained 300%, meaning that a $1,000 investment grew to $4,000. Annualized, that's a return of 14.9%. Figure 5-1 illustrates the effects of compounding on the S&P 500 stock-price index.

Although the average market returns with reinvested dividends are hefty, you would have done even better with some individual stocks. If ten years ago you had invested $1,000 in Abbott Laboratories, a maker of diversified health care products, and reinvested the dividends, you would have $5,922 for an annual return of 19%. A

Figure 5-1

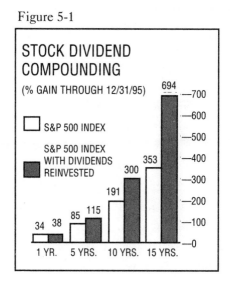

$1,000 investment ten years ago in PepsiCo (the well-known soft drink, snack foods, and restaurant company) would now be worth $8,126 with dividends plowed back. A real eye-popper is Home Depot, the big do-it-yourself retailer. If you had bought $1,000 worth of the stock a decade ago and reinvested the dividends, you'd now have $39,820, for an annual return of 45%. Table 5-2 lists companies in which $1,000 invested on December 31, 1985 grew in value to $6,200 or more, with dividends reinvested, on December 31, 1995.

Dividend Reinvestment Plans

More than 800 companies offer dividend reinvestment plans, or DRPs, which allow you to compound your dividends by investing them in additional shares of stock. For long-term investors, DRPs are a convenient and low-cost way to build a stock portfolio. Even if you need the dividends to live on, you can still participate in the plans. Many DRPs allow partial dividend reinvestment, whereby you can receive the dividends on a number of shares of your choosing and have the balance reinvested to buy more stock. A few plans allow you to sign up only for the optional cash payment feature (see below), which means you can receive all the dividends.

Stocks with current high dividends or growing dividends let your capital build faster. For example, Medtronic (a producer of cardiac pacemakers and mechanical heart valves) increased its dividend 103% over the five years from 1991 through 1995, with $1,000 invested at the end

Table 5-2. Stocks Posting Superior Returns with Reinvested Dividends. A $1,000 investment in any of the stocks would have grown to more than $6,200 over the last ten years. Each of these companies offers a dividend reinvestment plan (DRP).

Company	Ticker	$1,000 Became
Home Depot	HD	$39,820
Medtronic	MDT	22,395
Paychex, Inc.	PAYX	20,884
Computer Associates	CA	20,117
Federal National Mortgage	FNM	17,093
Gillette Co.	G	14,288
Cracker Barrel Old Country	CBRL	14,137
Wrigley, (Wm.) Jr.	WWY	12,770
Omnicare, Inc.	OCR	12,703
Coca-Cola Co.	KO	12,680
Countrywide Credit Indus.	CCR	12,479
Intel Corp.	INTC	11,774
Philip Morris Cos.	MO	11,491
Washington Mutual	WAMU	10,870
UST, Inc.	UST	10,754
Merck & Co.	MRK	10,605
Nordson Corp.	NDSN	10,343
Crompton & Knowles	CNK	10,320
Franklin Resources	BEN	9,990
Lancaster Colony	LANC	9,934
Wells Fargo	WFC	9,784
Century Telephone	CTL	9,613
Schering-Plough	SGP	9,463
Albertson's, Inc.	ABS	9,363
Kennametal, Inc.	KMT	9,353
Federal Signal	FSS	9,164
Norwest Corp.	NOB	8,951
First Commercial Corp.	FCLR	8,481

Table 5-2. Stocks Posting Superior Returns with Reinvested Dividends. *(cont'd)*

Company	Ticker	$1,000 Became
Phelps Dodge	PD	8,358
PepsiCo, Inc.	PEP	8,126
Johnson & Johnson	JNJ	7,858
Illinois Tool Works	ITW	7,641
Mattel, Inc.	MAT	7,639
First Empire State	FES	7,422
Telephone & Data Systems	TDS	7,394
Merry Land & Investment	MRY	7,313
Interpublic Group	IPG	7,246
Fifth Third Bancorp	FITB	7,241
Cincinnati Bell	CSN	7,207
Monsanto Co.	MTC	7,084
Reynolds & Reynolds	REY	6,994
CPC International	CPC	6,911
Caterpillar, Inc.	CAT	6,889
McCormick & Co.	MCCRK	6,793
Nucor Corp.	NUE	6,769
Loctite Corp.	LOC	6,697
Arnold Indus	AIND	6,664
Glaxo Wellcome plc ADR	GLX	6,656
Kimberly-Clark	KMB	6,605
Tyco International	TYC	6,547
Motorola, Inc.	MOT	6,541
Pfizer, Inc.	PFE	6,453
ALLTEL Corp.	AT	6,424
Lukens, Inc.	LUC	6,405
Donaldson Co.	DCI	6,360
Sara Lee Corp.	SLE	6,322
SBC Communications	SBC	6,282
Hercules, Inc.	HPC	6,208

of 1985 worth $22,395 on December 31, 1995, a 36% annual rate of return. Motorola's dividend, which is up 111% in five years, helped the stock attain a 21% annual rate of return over the 1985–1995 period.

Many brokers will now reinvest dividends for you on any stock without a fee. They do not, however, permit you to take advantage of a DRP's optional cash purchase feature. This valuable feature permits you to send in money (usually, the minimum amount is low and the maximum is fairly high) on a periodic basis to purchase shares at little or no transaction cost.

Another valuable aspect of some DRPs is the reinvestment of dividends at a discount from the market price. More than 90 companies offer a discount, ranging from 1% to 10%. Most are banks and utilities, which need a large amount of capital to conduct their businesses. DRPs are an inexpensive way for these companies to raise capital (new shares are issued for the plans rather than purchased from the open market). For a list of companies offering discounts, see Table 5-3.

Of course, you can also receive the benefits of compounding via mutual funds. Funds—both open-end (which continuously issue shares to accommodate new investors or existing investors who are adding money to their accounts) and closed-end (which have a relatively fixed number of shares that trade on the open market as any other stocks)—offer shareholders the option of reinvesting dividends, as well as any capital gains distributions.

Table 5-3. DRP Stocks Offering Discounts

Company/Ticker	Where Traded	Discount %
ADAC Laboratories/ADAC	NASDAQ	5
American Water Works/AWK	NYSE	5
Aquarion/WTR	NYSE	5
Atmos Energy/ATO	NYSE	3
Ball Corp./BLL	NYSE	5
Bank of Boston/BKB	NYSE	3
Banponce Corp./BPOP	NASDAQ	5
Bay View Capital/BVFS	NASDAQ	5
Berkshire Gas/BGAS	NASDAQ	3, 3*
Blount Inc./BLT.A	NYSE	5
Bradley REIT/BTR	NYSE	3, 3*
Burnham Pac. Prop./BPP	NYSE	5
Calif. Financial Holding/CFHC	NASDAQ	3
Calif Water Service/CWT	NYSE	3
Capstead Mortgage/CMO	NYSE	3, 3*
Carolina First Corp./CAFC	NASDAQ	5
CNB Bancshares/BNK	NYSE	3
Colonial Gas/CGES	NASDAQ	5
Columbus Realty Trust/CLB	NASDAQ	5
Connecticut Water Service/CTWS	NASDAQ	5
Countrywide Credit/CCR	NYSE	4
Cousins Property/CUZ	NYSE	5
Crestar Financial/CF	NYSE	5
Duke Realty Invest./DRE	NYSE	4
Empire District Electric/EDE	NYSE	5
Energynorth Inc./EI	NYSE	5
Essex County Gas/ECGC	NASDAQ	5
E'Town/ETW	NYSE	5
First American Corp.-Tenn/FATN	NASDAQ	5
First Commerce/FCOM	NASDAQ	5
First Commercial Corp./FCLR	NASDAQ	5

Company/Ticker	Where Traded	Discount %
First Michigan Bank/FMBC	NASDAQ	5
First of America Bank/FOA	NYSE	5
First Union/FTU	NYSE	1, 1*
Fleming Cos./FLM	NYSE	5
Fuller (H.B.)/FULL	NASDAQ	3
Goodmark Foods/GDMK	NASDAQ	1, 2*
Green Mountain Power/GMP	NYSE	5
Hibernia Corp./HIB	NYSE	5
Household International/HI	NYSE	2 1/2
Huntington Bancshares/HBAN	NASDAQ	5
Independent Bank Corp./IBCP	NASDAQ	5
IPL Energy/IPPIF	NASDAQ	5
IRT Property/IRT	NYSE	5
IWC Resources/IWCR	NASDAQ	3, 3*
Kennametal/KMT	NYSE	5
Lafarge Corp./LAF	NYSE	5
Media General/MEG.A	ASE	5
Mercantile Bancshares/MRBK	NASDAQ	5
Merry Land & Investments/MRY	NYSE	5, 5*
National City Corp./NCC	NYSE	3, 3*
New Plan Realty Trust/NPR	NYSE	5
Old National Bancorp/OLDB	NASDAQ	3, 3*
Oneok/OKE	NYSE	3
Philadelphia Suburban/PSC	NYSE	5
Piccadilly Cafeterias/PIC	NYSE	5
Piedmont Natural Gas/PNY	NYSE	5, 5*
Presidential Realty/PDL.B	ASE	5
Public Service Co. of N.C./PGS	NYSE	5
Second Bancorp/SECD	NASDAQ	5, 5*
Southern National/SNB	NYSE	3
Southwest Water/SWWC	NASDAQ	5
Telephone & Data Systems/TDS	NYSE	5

Table 5-3. DRP Stocks Offering Discounts *(cont'd)*

Company/Ticker	Where Traded	Discount %
Time Warner/TWX	NYSE	5
Timken/TKR	NYSE	5
Total Petroleum/TPN	NYSE	5
Transcanada Pipelines/TRP	NYSE	5
Union Planters/UPC	NYSE	5
United Cities Gas/UCIT	NASDAQ	5
United Mobile Homes/UMH	ASE	5
Unitil Corp./UTL	NYSE	5
Unocal Corp./UCL	NYSE	3
USX-U.S. Steel/X	NYSE	3, 3*
Utilicorp United/UCU	NYSE	5
Valley Resources/VR	ASE	5
Washington National/WNT	NYSE	5
Wells Fargo/WFC	NYSE	3
Westcoast Energy/WE	NYSE	5
York Financial/YFED	NASDAQ	10

*Discount on optional cash payments.

IRAs and Compounding

The magic of compounding works especially well with an Individual Retirement Account (IRA). A person who contributes $2,000 annually (the maximum allowed, unless one has a non-working spouse, in which case the maximum is $2,250) will accumulate $297,200 after thirty years, assuming a 9% annual return (stocks historically have returned an average of 10% annually). In a taxable account, assuming a 28% tax rate, the amount would be only $183,300.

If you fund an IRA partially or entirely with appreciating stocks that don't pay dividends, the tax-deferred compounding advantage may be significantly offset by the loss of capital gains tax treatment when it comes time to take distributions. Your IRA withdrawals are taxed as ordinary income. You can start distributing at age 59½ if you wish, but the first distribution must be made by April 1 of the year after you reach age 70½ and the second by December 31 of that year. The minimum IRA distribution can be based on the combined life expectancies of the IRA owner and a younger designated beneficiary, and during such a span, Congress could easily increase the tax bite on ordinary income and/or diminish the capital gains tax break. Another disadvantage of funding an IRA with stocks: You can't deduct investment losses realized in the account. Without that restriction, IRAs would be ideal for investors who trade stocks frequently, incurring losses as well as short-term gains that would otherwise be taxed at ordinary income rates. However, by holding IRA stocks for long periods, ten years or more, you substantially reduce the risk of incurring nondeductible losses in the account.

Dividend-Paying Stocks in IRAs

High-yield stocks and particularly stocks with steadily increasing dividends are good IRA funding choices for most investors. For accounts that will remain largely undistributed for fifteen or twenty years or longer, portfolios consisting entirely of dividend-paying stocks with growth potential can be expected to outperform portfolios balanced with stocks and fixed-income investments. The tax deferral not only accelerates dividend yield compounding, it also postpones taxes when you sell long-time holdings with huge gains—and then spreads the tax bite over your distribution years.

A convenient way to set up a self-directed IRA is via dividend reinvestment plans. At this writing, twelve companies currently permit such IRAs, and the list is growing. In order to have stocks in a self-directed IRA, you must have an account custodian. Brokerage houses normally won't offer to act as a custodian for an IRA with a DRP since they don't get commissions when stocks are purchased in a plan. Companies now offering the IRA option are: Atmos Energy (1-800-382-8667), Barnett Banks (1-800-328-5822), Centerior Energy (1-800-433-7794), Connecticut Energy (1-800-736-3001), Connecticut Water (1-800-426-5523), Exxon (1-800-252-1800), GTE Corp. (1-800-225-5160), Mobil (1-800-648-9291), Morton International (1-800-990-1010), Portland General (1-800-446-2617), SBC Communications (formerly Southwestern Bell) (1-800-351-7221), and UtiliCorp United (1-800-487-6661).

The question often arises whether it pays to contribute to an IRA if you cannot deduct the contributions on your income tax return. Unless you're not covered by a qualified pension plan or are a relatively low-income taxpayer (no more than $40,000 on joint returns or $25,000 on single returns), you'll get no deduction for IRA contributions. But even if you can't deduct your funding, it still pays to set up an IRA. Invested in dividend-paying growth stocks or mutual funds, $2,000 can, compounded tax-free, create a sizable nest egg. And although there is some paperwork involved (you must file

IRS Form 8606, "Nondeductible IRA Contributions, IRA Basis, and Nontaxable IRA Distributions" with your income tax return), it is far from burdensome.

Summing Up

1. *Compounding truly is magic. Your investment grows as it earns returns on the initial money invested and on the interest or dividends added.*

2. *To find out quickly how long it would take to double your money at different rates, use the "Rule of 72." Just divide 72 by the yield.*

3. *If you reinvest your dividends via dividend reinvestment plans, your stake in a particular company can grow dramatically over time. If you need some income, most DRPs allow you to put only some of your shares into the plans.*

4. *Individual retirement accounts (IRAs) receive an extra lift from compounding because they grow tax-free until withdrawal.*

5. *Dividend-paying stocks are excellent choices for IRAs.*

6. *Even if you can't deduct your IRA contributions on your income tax return, they are still worthwhile.*

Dividend **6** Investing via Mutual Funds

It's safe to say that, were it not for mutual funds, millions of people of modest means would not have enjoyed the benefits of equity investing. As we pointed out earlier, stocks have outperformed other types of investments over the long term by a good margin. Enthusiasm for funds has spilled over to more affluent investors, who regard mutual funds, rightly so, as a good way to diversify their portfolios.

Reflecting their popularity, the mutual fund industry has mushroomed from sixty-eight funds in 1940 (when Congress passed the Investment Company Act) to almost 6,000 in 1995. Assets have rocketed from $448 million in 1940 to nearly $3 trillion. According to the Investment Company Institute, the trade group for the fund industry, more than 38 million individuals, or 31% of U.S. households, own mutual funds. Some expect that by the year 2000, individuals will have more money in mutual finds than in bank savings accounts and CDs.

Besides their relatively low purchase minimums and the fact that subsequent small sums may be added on a regular basis, mutual funds offer the smaller investor diversification, which reduces risk. An added plus is professional management for those who don't have the time or inclination to look after their own portfolios. Although the pros don't often outperform the market, many do a creditable job.

Funds for the Dividend-Oriented

Income investors can choose various mutual funds that invest in money market instruments, bonds, and/or preferred stocks (fixed-income funds) or in a combination of stocks and bonds (balanced funds). These funds' main objective is income, with capital gains a secondary consideration. For those looking for a combination of income and capital appreciation, two fund categories fit the bill: growth and income funds and equity income funds.

Growth and Income

This type of fund aims for steady, if not high, income payouts, while placing equal weight on capital appreciation. Many of the stocks in the S&P 500 index can be found in growth and income funds. The majority of the funds are large-cap portfolios with various percentages in different industries (known as sector weightings). Growth and income funds are less susceptible to short-term economic-cycle and sector shifts. Morningstar, which ranks mutual funds, defines growth and income funds as those that seek growth of capital and current income as near-equal objectives, primarily by investing in equity securities with above-average yields and some potential for appreciation.

Equity Income

Equity income funds seek relatively high current income and growth of income by investing 60% or more of their portfolios in equities. Risk is generally low. Managers of equity income funds generally attempt to provide yields that are at least 50% higher than the yield of the S&P 500. Big dividend payers, such as the major oil companies, drugs, and utilities, can be found in the typical equity income portfolio. Morningstar's definition of an equity income fund is one that seeks income by investing at least 65% of its assets in equity securities with above-average yields.

Despite the conservative nature of growth and income funds and equity income funds, a 1995 study by investment advisor T. Rowe Price Associates and Lipper Analytical Services (which compiles statistics on mutual fund performance) shows that, over the past twenty-five years, equity income funds, with dividends reinvested, rose 10.7% a year, while growth and income funds gained 10.6% annually. That compares with growth funds, which were up 10.1% in the same period and small-cap funds, which rose less than 10%. The higher returns of the dividend-oriented funds, moreover, were achieved with fewer down years and less-steep drops than small-stock funds.

On a cumulative basis, according to Lipper Analytical Services, over the past thirty-five years, growth and income funds were up 3,800% and equity income funds jumped 4,053%, compared with 2,312% for capital appreciation funds and 3,291% for growth funds. Again, the tortoise beats the hare!

Before we talk about specific growth and income and equity income funds, a word on load vs. no-load funds is in order. We believe unequivocally that no-load funds are your best bet. Your broker, of course, will not agree. By buying a fund with no sales charge, you are not only saving on the commission, but all of your money goes into the fund as well. For example, $10,000 invested in an 8.5% front-end load fund results in an $850 sales charge and only a $9,150 investment in the fund. The load actually represents 9.3% of the net funds invested. If a load fund is held for many years, the effect of the load, if paid up front, is not diminished as quickly as many believe. If the money paid for the load had been working for you, as in a no-load fund, it would have been compounding over the entire period.

Some experts say load vs. no-load isn't an important issue, and that the key to picking a fund is performance. We maintain that for every strong-performing load fund, there is a similar no-load or low-load fund.

Keep in mind that funds have various ways of tacking on sales charges. At one time, an 8.5% front-end sales commission was common. Currently the number of funds charging the full 8.5% load is diminishing. Some funds sold by brokerage firms have lowered their front-end commissions to 4% or less, and others have introduced back-end loads, deferred sales charges, or redemption fees, all of which mean you pay when you sell the fund. The 12b-1 fee, named for the section of the Investment Company Act that permits it, has also become popular. It allows the fund's investment advisor to use fund assets to pay for distribution costs, including advertising, distribution of fund literature, and sales commissions paid to brokers.

Some funds use 12b-1 fees as load charges in disguise. Since the charge is annual and based on the value of the investments, a high 12b-1 fee can result in total costs to long-term investors that are higher than the old 8.5% up-front sales load, yet allowing the fund to be classified as no-load. Make sure you check the fund prospectus for any charges that are imposed.

The current trend among mutual funds is to build assets, since management fees are based on a percentage of a fund's total assets. Thus, an increasing number of funds have tried to gather more assets by reducing front-end charges.

Favored Growth and Income Funds

The following growth and income funds have good long-term performance records and impose no sales charges or other fees, except for management fees.

- **AARP Growth & Income Fund** emphasizes high-yield stocks to meet its goal of capital growth and current income. It picks stocks on the basis of relative dividend yields rather than on price-to-earnings or price-to-book ratios. The fund only buys stocks whose yields are at least 20% higher than that of the S&P 500 index. An issue is sold when its dividend yield drops below 75% of the S&P 500's yield. The fund is often invested in out-of-favor stocks and industries and has shown low volatility over the years.

  Five-year average annual return (through December 1995): 16.8%

  Management fee: 0.54%

  Minimum initial investment: $500

  Telephone: 1-800-322-2282

- **Babson Value Fund** follows a value-oriented investment strategy. The fund looks for undervalued stocks, using price-to-book and price-earnings measures. The portfolio usually is made up of stocks that are out of favor with investors. Issues are weighted equally. If one holding rises by more than 20%, it is cut back to its original allocation. The average price-earnings multiple in the portfolio is among the lowest in the growth and income fund category.

  Five-year average annual return (through December 1995): 19.8%

  Management fee: 0.95%

  Minimum initial investment: $1,000

  Telephone: 1-800-422-2766

- **Dodge & Cox Stock Fund** invests in companies that are currently out of favor. The fund looks for companies that have the potential for positive earnings surprises. A "bottom-up," or company-specific, approach is used. Stocks in the portfolio have below-average price-earnings ratios, price-to-book ratios, and market-capitalization-to-sales ratios. Investments are made with at least a three- to five-year time horizon, and the turnover rate is low.
  Five-year average annual return (through December 1995): 17.4%
  Management fee: 0.50%.
  Minimum initial investment: $2,500
  Telephone: 1-800-621-3979

- **Fidelity Growth & Income Fund** seeks long-term capital growth, current income, and growth of income consistent with reasonable risk. It invests primarily in securities of companies that pay current dividends and offer potential earnings growth. Generally, the fund sells stocks with dividends that fall below the yield of the S&P 500 index. The fund may invest up to 35% of assets in debt securities rated below BBB by Standard & Poor's. It employs a bottom-up strategy, buying stocks that are inexpensive relative to their historical price-earnings ratios and price-to-cash flow ratios.
  Five-year average annual return (through December 1995): 21.2%
  Management fee: 0.52%
  Minimum initial investment: $2,500
  Telephone: 1-800-544-8888

- **Invesco Value Equity Fund** seeks above-average capital appreciation and current income via investments primarily in common stocks. It uses a bottom-up approach, screening companies in the S&P 500 index, in addition to 300 large- and mid-cap companies, for undervalued situations, and tends to invest in out-of-favor groups. The fund's downside risk is limited by avoiding large sector commitments.
  Five-year average annual return (through December 1995): 16.4%
  Management fee: 0.75%
  Minimum initial investment: $1,000
  Telephone: 1-800-525-8085

- **Lexington Corporate Leaders Fund** seeks long-term capital growth and income. The fund is unusual in that, at its inception in 1935 the advisor, Lexington Management Corp., selected a group of thirty blue chip companies to comprise a permanent portfolio, holding an equal number of shares of each company. If a stock splits, those shares are sold and redistributed among the other positions in the portfolio. The fund is barred from adding new positions. The only exception is in the case of a spinoff, of which there has been only one in almost sixty years. Seven of its original thirty companies have been eliminated because they no longer meet the fund's investment criteria (they either stopped paying dividends or else were no longer listed on the New York Stock Exchange). The portfolio includes one of the largest mutual-fund positions in AT&T.

Five-year average annual return (through December 1995): 16.3%
Management fee: 0.35%
Minimum initial investment: $1,000
Telephone: 1-800-526-0056

- **Mutual Qualified Fund** seeks capital appreciation, with income as a secondary goal. The fund looks for stocks that are trading at large discounts to book value. It also invests in stocks of companies involved in prospective mergers, consolidations, liquidations, or other special situations. These investments may not comprise more than 50% of assets.

  Five-year average annual return (through December 1995): 19.5%
  Management fee: 0.60%
  Minimum initial investment: $1,000
  Telephone: 1-800-553-3014

  Note: This fund recently adopted a sales charge, but grandfathered existing no-load shareholders. We recommend it only for those who can buy the fund without a sales charge.

- **Scudder Growth & Income Fund** seeks capital growth and current income through high-yielding stocks. The fund believes that a stock's yield is a better valuation tool than its price-earnings ratio. As a result, many of the issues are out of investor favor. Stocks are purchased only when yields are at least 20% higher than that of the S&P 500 index. A stock will be sold when its yield falls to 75%

of that of the S&P 500 index. The fund's emphasis on yield has resulted in solid returns and below-average risk.
Five-year average annual return (through December 1995): 16.9%
Management fee: 0.60%
Minimum initial investment: $1,000
Telephone: 1-800-225-2470

- **T. Rowe Price Growth & Income** seeks long-term growth of capital, current income, and an increase in future income. The fund invests most of its assets in stocks of companies with earnings that are sufficient to support a growing dividend. Up to 30% of assets may be invested in convertible and corporate debt securities and preferred stocks. A strict value approach is used, with high-growth issues generally avoided. Overweighting in a particular sector is also avoided.
Five-year average annual return (through December 1995): 17.5%
Management fee: 0.60%
Minimum initial investment: $2,500
Telephone: 1-800-638-5660

- **Vanguard Quantitative** seeks a total return greater than that of the S&P 500 index. The fund has a diversified portfolio similar to the S&P 500 in terms of dividend yield, price-earnings ratio, return on equity, and price-to-book ratio. At least 65% of assets are invested in securities that are included in the S&P 500. The fund emphasizes conservatism. It seeks to achieve consistent positive returns while avoiding large losses during market downturns.

Five-year average annual return (through December 1995): 16.5%

Management fee: 0.25%

Minimum initial investment: $3,000

Telephone: 1-800-662-7447

Favored Equity Income Funds

The following equity income funds boast above-average performance records and carry no sales charges or other fees, except for management fees.

- **Fidelity Equity Income II** invests at least 65% of its assets in dividend-paying stocks. A value-oriented fund, Fidelity Equity Income II looks for issues that have relatively low price-earnings and price-to-book ratios. Financial stocks normally make up a large chunk of the portfolio. Foreign stocks are also heavily weighted in the portfolio.

  Five-year average annual return (through December 1995): 21.8%

  Management fee: 0.52%

  Minimum initial investment: $2,500

  Telephone: 1-800-544-8888

- **Hotchkis & Wiley Equity Income**'s portfolio generally consists of more common stocks than those of most of its peers. Few bonds and convertible bonds are bought. Issues are selected on the basis of strong earnings growth and healthy balance sheets. High quality, large-cap stocks are the order of the day. The fund is somewhat more volatile than its peers.

Five-year average annual return (through December 1995): 18.2%

Management fee: 0.75%

Minimum initial investment: $5,000 (IRAs: $1,000)

Telephone: 1-800-346-7301

- **T. Rowe Price Equity Income** seeks high current income and capital appreciation by investing primarily in dividend-paying stocks of well-established companies. The balance of assets are invested in preferred stocks or investment-grade fixed-income securities. Large-capitalization stocks that are undervalued or out of favor figure prominently.

  Five-year average annual return (through December 1995): 18%

  Management fee: 0.50%

  Minimum initial investment: $2,500

  Telephone: 1-800-638-5660

- **T. Rowe Price Dividend Growth Fund** seeks to provide increasing dividend income and long-term capital appreciation. The fund invests primarily in established, well-managed companies whose earnings and dividends have grown steadily over the years and are expected to continue to do so. In operation only since 1992, the fund has recorded an above-average return.

Three-year average annual return (through December 1995): 17.1%
Management fee: 0.23%
Minimum investment: $2,500
Telephone: 1-800-638-5660

- **Vanguard Equity Income Fund** aims to provide its investors with yields above that of the S&P 500. The fund concentrates on well-established, large-capitalization stocks that are out of investor favor, though the companies' fundamentals and finances are strong enough to support their dividends.
Five-year average annual return (through December 1995): 16.2%
Management fee: 0.24%
Minimum initial investment: $3,000
Telephone: 1-800-662-7447

Closed-End Funds

Unlike open-end mutual funds that issue and redeem shares at net asset value, or NAV (the total market value of all stocks held divided by the number of fund shares outstanding), closed-end funds don't redeem shares. They increase shares outstanding only when raising new capital through secondary offerings, and they can buy back shares on the open market. Since supply and demand determine their share prices, closed-end funds may sell at discounts or premiums to NAV. The funds are traded like individual stocks on the exchanges and over-the-counter.

With closed-end funds, managements are not forced to sell low as investors exit a falling market or buy high with new money. These funds can take a longer-term view than mutual funds that are subject to net redemptions, and they can also hold illiquid stocks that might put other funds in a bind.

Three closed-end funds that have large-cap dividend-oriented stock portfolios with moderate expense ratios and that sell at discounts are **Adams Express, Tri-Continental Corp.**, and **Nations Balanced Target Fund.** Nations Balanced aims to return principal by maintaining half the portfolio in zero-coupon Treasury notes; the other half is in blue chip stocks. The fund matures on September 30, 2004, when management expects to return at least the $10 per share provided by original investors who reinvest all dividends and hold to maturity.

The financial pages of newspapers generally list closed-end fund NAVs only weekly, but the major closed-end funds calculate NAV daily, and provide it as part of a toll-free phone service. A separate listing of closed-end funds can be found in *Standard & Poor's Stock Guide*. The listing offers uniform data on more than 500 closed-end funds in twenty-four investment categories.

Summing Up

1. *Mutual funds are a good way for smaller dividend-oriented investors to invest. Funds also are attractive for larger investors because they offer diversification.*

2. *Growth and income funds and equity income funds are the two major categories of funds for those mainly interested in dividend income.*

3. *Although growth and income funds and equity income funds are conservative and carry relatively small risk, they have done better than more aggressive, riskier funds over the past twenty-five years.*

4. *We recommend you buy only no-load (no sales charge) funds. By purchasing funds that don't have sales charges, not only do you save on the commission, but all of your money goes into the fund as well. We also recommend you avoid funds that have 12b-1 fees and other charges.*

5. *Favored growth and income funds are AARP Growth & Income Fund, Babson Value Fund, Dodge & Cox Stock Fund, Fidelity Growth & Income Fund, Invesco Value Equity Fund, Lexington Corporate Leaders Fund, Scudder Growth & Income Fund, T. Rowe Price Growth & Income Fund, and Vanguard Quantitative. Favored equity income funds are Fidelity Equity Income II, Hotchkis & Wiley Equity Income, T. Rowe Price Equity Income Fund, T. Rowe Price Dividend Growth Fund, and Vanguard Equity Fund.*

6. *Consider conservative, blue chip, closed-end funds that sell at a discount. Examples are: Adams Express, Tri-Continental, and Nations Balanced Target.*

Dividend 7 Strategies

In Chap. 5, we took a look at how reinvesting dividends can fatten your portfolio over time. We spoke about how dividend reinvestment is convenient and low-cost. Another benefit of reinvesting your dividends is that it allows you to take advantage of dollar-cost-averaging. This is one of several strategies we'll examine in this chapter.

Dollar-Cost-Averaging

Every investor is looking for an easy way to do well in the market. Dollar-cost-averaging is perhaps the best known "easy" or mechanical way to invest. The strategy offers you the potential for profits with reduced market risk. It frees you of the problems of attempting to time market fluctuations, and, in fact, puts those swings to work for you.

Dollar-cost-averaging simply entails buying a fixed dollar amount of a stock at specific time intervals. You buy fewer shares when the price is high and more shares when it is low. Over the years, your average cost per share using this formula method of investing will be lower than the average of your purchase prices, providing the stock is in a basic long-term uptrend.

See Table 7-1 for an example of how dollar-cost-averaging works. If you invest $600 a month for three months and the purchase price of the stock for each of the three months is $25, $20, and $30 a share, respectively, your total investment of $1,800 buys 74 shares at an average cost of $24.32 a share (before commissions). If you had invested the $1,800 in a lump sum at the average price of $25, you would have bought only 72 shares. The advantage would have been the same had the price pattern been $30, $25, $20; $20, $25, $30; or $20, $30, $25.

Table 7-1. Dollar-Cost-Averaging

Months	Investment	Share Price	Number of Shares
1	$600	$25	24
2	600	20	30
3	600	30	20
		$25 Avg. Price	
	Total: $1,800		74 shares
Average cost per share: $1,800/74 = $24.32			

Dollar-cost-averaging enables you to turn the market's movements to your advantage over a period of time. Overall, you should achieve solid long-term investment results. Remember, though, the key to success is "stick-to-itiveness." Don't be scared off when the market is in a downtrend. Regard a period of falling stock prices as an opportunity to buy a larger number of shares of an issue that will likely climb in the not-too-distant future.

Stocks that pay dividends and have a history of regularly increasing payments are especially good for dollar-cost-averaging. This type of stock can help to provide a regular money flow for periodic investments, particularly when you have an unexpectedly large bill due that makes it difficult to come up with the money you need to invest. To get the most out of your dollar-cost-averaging plan, you should start to invest before a stock sells ex-dividend (the buyer of a stock selling ex-dividend, meaning without the dividend, does not receive the recently declared dividend; rather, the payment goes to the seller). Check *Standard & Poor's Stock Guide* for ex-dividend dates.

Dow Dividend Strategy

Another formula investing method that has proven itself over the years is the Dow dividend strategy, or the Dogs of the Dow, as *Barron's* calls it. The strategy is simplicity itself. At the end of every year, buy the ten highest-yielding stocks of the thirty in the Dow Jones Industrial Average, putting equal amounts of money into the ten issues. Hold the stocks until the end of the following year, and repeat the process.

The strategy historically has done better than the Dow Jones Industrial Average as a whole. Over the past 60 years, the Dow dividend strategy has not only outperformed the Dow index and the S&P 500, but also just about every other investment strategy. According to O'Shaughnessy Capital Management, a money management company based in Greenwich, Connecticut, $10,000 invested on December 31, 1928 in the ten-highest yielding stocks in the Dow annually rebalanced (replacing stocks that no longer qualified with those that did) would have been worth $26,884,667 on December 31, 1995. By comparison, $10,000 invested in the S&P 500 index in that period would have been worth $4,996,898. The strategy works well even in bad markets. In the worst market period since World War II (1973–1974), the ten top-yielding Dow stocks were up slightly vs. a 40% plunge in the S&P 500.

You can find a list of the stocks in the Dow Industrials in *The Wall Street Journal*. The paper runs the names in the daily market chart in Section C. At this writing, the thirty issues in the index are the following:

AT&T	Goodyear
AlliedSignal	IBM
Aluminum Co. of America	International Paper
American Express	McDonald's Corp.
Bethlehem Steel	Merck & Co.
Boeing	Minnesota Mining & Mfg.

Caterpillar Inc.	Morgan (J.P.)
Chevron	Philip Morris
Coca-Cola	Procter & Gamble
Disney (Walt)	Sears, Roebuck
DuPont	Texaco
Eastman Kodak	Union Carbide
Exxon	United Technologies
General Electric	Westinghouse
General Motors	Woolworth

At the end of 1995, the top ten Dow yielders were: Caterpillar, Chevron, DuPont, Exxon, General Electric, International Paper, J.P. Morgan, Minnesota Mining & Manufacturing, Philip Morris, and Texaco.

What's the Secret?

Why does the Dow dividend strategy work so well? Perhaps it's because the prices of the highest-yielding stocks in the Dow are depressed. More often than not, however, the issues offer good value. They are all well-known, large-capitalization stocks of companies that, for the most part, are not likely to go out of business. Usually, company-specific problems that have caused investors to shun the stocks can be fixed. Or it may be just a question of time before unfavorable industry conditions can be reversed, such as high interest rates that would adversely affect financial stocks or a recession that would depress cyclical stocks.

In the meantime, you are receiving above-average dividend yields. (Even though Woolworth, one of the Dow top yielders for 1994, omitted its dividend in April 1995, investors in the Dow dividend strategy still received a solid average yield from the other nine stocks.) Keep in mind that dividends have historically accounted for more than 40% of the average total return on all of the Dow stocks.

Variations on a Theme

Some variations on the Dow dividend strategy have sprung up. One is the "Flying Five," in which you buy the five lowest-priced stocks among the ten Dow high yielders. This approach has actually done better than the top ten approach. According to O'Shaughnessy Capital Management, the "Flying Five" has returned an average 16.5% from December 31, 1928 to December 31, 1995, compared with the 14.7% return of the top ten strategy. This variation, however, carries more risk, since you don't have as much diversification as with the top ten Dow yielders.

There is also the strategy that calls for buying only the five top-yielding stocks in the Dow. The return on the top five since 1928—14.6%—about matches that of the top-yielding ten stocks. Here again, you are less diversified.

The riskiest variation is called the "Penultimate Profit Prospect," in which you buy only the second-lowest-priced issue (who knows why the second-lowest priced rather than another number) among the Dow's ten highest-yielding stocks. Needless to say, if you're a conservative long-term investor who believes in diversification and likes to sleep at night, the "three Ps" technique is not for you.

The polar extreme of the Penultimate Profit Prospect is the Cornerstone Value approach promoted by Jim O'Shaughnessy, head of O'Shaughnessy Capital Management. He advocates buying the shares of fifty large, well-known companies with the highest dividend yields. That's like starting your own mutual fund. Obviously not for the small investor, the strategy nevertheless resulted in a 14.6% average annual return from 1954 to 1995, compared with a 10.7% gain in the S&P 500.

The Dow Dividend Strategy via UITs

The Dow dividend strategy has proven so popular that a number of brokerage houses now offer unit investment trusts based on the strategy. (Unit investment trusts, in contrast to continually managed mutual funds, are unmanaged fixed portfolios of stocks or bonds that are held for a specified term.) Offered by Merrill Lynch, Smith Barney, Prudential Securities, PaineWebber and Dean Witter, the UITs are called the Select Ten portfolio. The UITs are invested in the ten highest-yielding Dow stocks and then turned over twelve months later. Small investors might consider the Select Ten UITs, since they can be purchased for as little as $1,000, or $250 for IRAs. Although there are fees (typically a 1% sales charge and 1.75% in annual management fees), they are much lower than what it would cost you to buy small amounts of stocks in ten companies from a broker.

Geraldine Weiss' Theory

Editor and publisher of the newsletter *Investment Quality Trends* (twice-monthly, $275 a year, phone 619-459-3818), Geraldine Weiss has for 30 years been championing the theory that a stock's underlying value is in its dividends, not in its earnings. She emphasizes that blue chip companies are more predictable than are newcomers or companies with erratic records of earnings and dividends. A blue chip is defined as stock of a company that (1) has raised its dividend at least five times in the past twelve years, (2) has at least five million shares outstanding, (3) has at least eighty institutions holding its stock, (4) has seen earnings improve in at least seven of the last twelve years, (5) has a record of at least twenty-five years of uninterrupted dividends, and (6) has a Standard & Poor's ranking of A or higher.

According to Ms. Weiss' theory, a stock's price is driven by its yield. When a stock offers a high dividend yield, investors will buy, which results in a higher price and a lower dividend yield. When the yield declines, the stock will languish until it falls far enough to make the yield attractive again.

Ms. Weiss' research has shown that stocks typically fluctuate between extremes of high dividend yield and low dividend yield. These recurring extremes can be used to establish a channel of undervalued and overvalued prices. The tops and bottoms of cycles are determined by charting the dividend yield of a stock over a long enough period of time for the dividend-yield pattern to emerge. By calculating the historic points at which a stock turns down, or reverses a slide and turns up, the future behavior of that stock can be anticipated. Ms. Weiss runs charts of many stocks in her books, *The Dividend Connection* (Dearborn Financial Publishing, Inc., 1995) and *Dividends Don't Lie* (Longman Financial Services Publishing, 1988).

Relative Dividend Yield

The relative dividend yield strategy, as espoused by Anthony Spare, a money manager based in San Francisco, is similar to Geraldine Weiss' technique. The two most common measures of whether a stock is overvalued or undervalued are the price-earnings ratio (the current price of the stock divided by its earnings per share for the last twelve months or estimated earnings for the next twelve months) and book value (assets minus liabilities). Instead, Spare's strategy calls for comparing the stock's dividend yield with the yield of the Standard & Poor's 500 index. If a stock's yield is considerably higher than that of the index, the stock is a buy.

To calculate the relative dividend yield, divide the yield of the S&P 500 into the stock's yield. When the relative dividend yield is well above 100%, it is a signal to buy the stock. As in the Dow dividend strategy and Ms. Weiss' approach, most of the stocks with buy signals are depressed and the companies are encountering difficulties, usually temporary. But the investor is compensated for being patient by a good dividend stream, as is the case with the other dividend strategies.

Summing Up

1. *Dollar-cost-averaging (buying a fixed-dollar amount of a stock at specific intervals) is a disciplined way to invest and makes market fluctuations work for you. Stocks that pay dividends and have a history of regularly increasing payments are especially good for this strategy, since they can help to provide a regular money flow for your periodic investing.*

2. *The Dow dividend strategy, in which you buy the ten highest-yielding stocks in the Dow Jones Industrial Average at the end of each year, has handily beaten the market over the past sixty years.*

3. *For small investors, Dow dividend strategy unit investment trusts (called the Select Ten) are a smart buy.*

4. *Variations on the Dow dividend strategy include buying the five lowest-priced stocks among the ten Dow high yielders, buying the top five Dow yielding stocks, or buying the top fifty large-capitalization stocks. All of these approaches have recorded impressive results.*

5. *Aids to determining when to buy or sell stocks are Geraldine Weiss' technique of dividend yield patterns or Anthony Spare's relative dividend yield (comparing a stock's yield with that of the Standard & Poor's 500 index).*

8

Profits from Dividend Cuts

$\mathbf{B}$ack in Chap. 2 we warned you never to buy a stock on the basis of its dividend yield alone. Nothing we will say in this chapter contradicts that basic rule. Remember that it's still important to look before you leap into an investment. Strange as it may seem, most people do more research before buying a refrigerator for a few hundred dollars than they do before buying a stock for several thousand dollars. But as we saw in the last chapter, higher yields can lead you to higher total returns simply by pointing you toward stocks that have become undervalued.

A Fear of Cuts

One reason that yields of some utility stocks are very high is that investors, believing that the dividends are in danger of being cut, simply avoid these issues. That may not always be a wise move. A twenty-year simulation for the period that ended February 28, 1992 pitted the five highest-yielding issues in the S&P utilities index against the broad market as represented by the S&P 500. The five highest-yielding utilities were "purchased" and held for a year. A stock was "sold" at the end of the holding period if it was no longer one of the top five in yield. Allowing for commissions of 1%, this trading approach to high-yielding utility stocks produced an annualized return of 13.2% vs. 11.4% for a "buy and hold" strategy using the S&P 500. Returns for both strategies are with dividends reinvested. If this sounds a bit like the methodology behind the Dow dividend strategy that we described in the last chapter, that's because it is. Both techniques rely on the market's tendency to overreact. In general, investors either "love" or "hate" a particular stock at any given time.

The utilities study was conducted by our colleague David Braverman, the manager of quantitative analysis at Standard & Poor's, and was published in S&P's weekly investment advisory newsletter, *The Outlook* on May 6, 1992. Braverman notes several general reasons that the total return of utilities was greater than that of the broad market over the twenty-year test. During periods of high inflation, many utilities are able to pass along a large portion of their increased operating costs to their customers. Yet, during recessions (there were four during the twenty-year period), commercial and industrial demand for power drops less than demand for cyclical goods such as steel. Consequently, earnings of utility companies are less volatile than those of many other industries.

Utility stocks also tend to behave differently at market extremes. In bull markets, they lag as investors chase stocks of companies that post strong earnings growth or bid up takeover candidates. In bear markets, however, the higher yields of utilities tend to provide support for the shares while other stocks tumble.

But why did the *highest-yielding* utilities beat the general market in the twenty-year simulation? When the market believes that a company is about to cut its dividend, it drives the price of the stock down. That, in turn, raises the current yield. There are really only two possibilities: The dividend is cut or it isn't. If it's cut soon after you purchase the stock, you'll probably suffer a paper loss as the value of the shares declines. On the other hand, if the dividend is trimmed after a long stretch of time, you will have had the benefit of an above-average yield for an extended period. The other possibility is that the dividend is never cut. In this case, you will have collected an above-average yield and probably will have seen a large capital gain once the market realizes that the risk of a dividend cut has passed.

Buying on the Cut

In his study, Braverman noted that a case could be made that a utility stock's rebound is faster if the dividend is reduced, since the lower payment to shareholders can help to improve the company's balance sheet and its financial flexibility. We decided to take a closer look at that idea by tracking the performance of electric companies that actually had cut their dividends.

As you might remember, in Chap. 1 we told you about FPL Group, a Florida-based electric utility holding company that cut its annual dividend from $2.48 to $1.68 in 1994, even though it had increased the payment annually for the preceding 48 years. We noted that the stock plunged almost 14% on the day of the announcement. What we didn't say was, had you bought FPL after that price decline and held it for a year, your investment would have appreciated 37%. And even with the reduced dividend, the total return for the year was well over 40%. Could this indicate a pattern among electric companies that cut their dividends?

To find out, we looked at major power companies that cut or omitted their dividends between 1985 and 1994. Right away, we discovered that omission of a dividend did not bode well for the utility's share price. Shares of four of the seven power companies that eliminated their dividend payments during that decade were lower a year later and posted an average loss of 57%. One stock was essentially unchanged and only two were higher in price. Our conclusion: You don't want to risk buying shares of an electric company in such bad shape that it must completely eliminate its dividend.

Table 8-1 shows the twenty-five dividend cuts by twenty-three electric utilities (Centerior Energy and New York State Electric & Gas each cut twice in the decade), arranged by date. If you had purchased the shares at the closing price on the day of the cut (or, if the cut was announced after the market close, at the closing price on the next trading day) and held it for a year, on only seven occasions (28% of the time) would you have lost money. The average loss was 24.2%. But on another four tries (16% of the time), the share price would have been essentially flat after a year. For this study, we defined flat as within $0.50 of the starting price.

That left fourteen gains in our study. Although the average share price appreciation was 23.3%, the chances of producing a gain (14 out of 25, or 56%) were little better than a coin toss.

Improving the Odds

Unless you thrive on casino-style risk, odds that are only slightly better than 50-50 are not worth your hard-earned money. But take a closer look at Table 8-1 and a pattern may start to emerge. Note that as the decade turned, more electric utility dividend cuts became profitable for people who bought after the announcement.

There were a dozen cuts from 1985 through 1989. Five of the stocks were lower a year later and another three were flat. In other words, you did not make a profit

Table 8-1. Electric Utilities That Cut Dividends 1985-1994

Dividend Cut Date	Stock	% Gain or Loss One Year Later
1994		
Oct. 14	New York State E&G	35.7
Aug. 16	TNP Enterprises	13.4
June 17	Edison International	24.5
May 9	FPL Group	37.0
Jan. 4	Centerior Energy	−29.4
1993		
Dec. 15	Central Maine Power	−16.0
Feb. 17	PacifiCorp	flat
1992		
Sept. 10	Unicom	27.0
July 10	Sierra Pacific Resources	18.4
1991		
June 18	Eastern Utilities Assoc.	19.0
1990		
Aug. 21	Ohio Edison	15.4
April 23	PECO Energy	28.6
Feb. 7	Portland General	6.0
1989		
Dec. 24	Boston Edison	flat
Aug. 22	Tucson Electric Pwr.	−53.7
1988		
Dec. 22	Pinnacle West Capital	−29.4
June 28	Pacific Gas & Electric	29.4
April 26	Pub. Ser. New Mexico	−27.3
March 22	Centerior Energy	flat
Jan. 15	New York State E&G	12.0

Dividend Cut Date	Stock	% Gain or Loss One Year Later
1987		
Dec. 18	Central Hudson G&E	14.0
Sept. 16	Rochester G&E	flat
July 23	Niagara Mohawk Pwr.	–6.7
1986		
April 18	DQE	–11.6
1985		
May 6	Kansas City P&L	45.9

in eight of twelve instances, or almost 67% of the time. Fast forward to the 1990s. Of the thirteen electric power companies that cut their dividends from 1990 through 1994, ten were higher in price a year later. That means people who bought on the dividend cut made a profit almost 77% of the time. Buying on the bad news worked much better in the 1990s than it did in the 1980s. Buy *why?*

One possible explanation is that the interest rate environment of the 1990s helped. Utility stocks are often considered "bond surrogates" and, like fixed-income securities, rise in value as interest rates decline. For most of the first three years of this decade, interest rates fell causing bonds and utility stocks to rise. Could this be the reason that even though the electric utilities in question cut their dividends, their share prices advanced?

Table 8-2 shows the ten electric utilities that rose in price after cutting their dividends between 1990 and 1994

Table 8-2. Performance of Dividend-cutting Electric Companies vs. S&P Utilities Index. Between 1990 and 1994, the ten electric utilities that cut their dividends and rose in price outpaced the utilities market in the year following the reduction.

Dividend Cut Date	Stock	% Gain One Year Later	% Gain in S&P Utilities Index	% Advantage of Stock over Index
1994				
Oct. 14	New York State E&G	35.7	19.7	81.0
Aug. 16	TNP Enterprises	13.4	7.6	76.0
June 17	Edison International	24.5	7.9	210.0
May 9	FPL Group	37.0	10.3	259.0
1992				
Sept. 10	Unicom	27.0	20.5	31.7
July 10	Sierra Pacific Resources	18.4	15.2	21.0
1991				
June 18	Eastern Utilities Assoc.	19.0	8.1	134.0
1990				
Aug. 21	Ohio Edison	15.4	7.6	102.0
April 23	PECO Energy	28.6	3.6	694.0
Feb. 7	Portland General	6.0	flat	...

and the change in value of the S&P utilities index over the same one-year periods. Nine of the ten stocks advanced when utility stock prices were rising. In one case, the index was virtually flat after a year. But in each of the ten cases, the share price performance of the company that had cut its dividend was better than the advance in the utilities index over the same period. While utilities in general went nowhere (as measured by the index), the shares of Portland General rose 6% for the year ended February 7, 1991. The outperformance was even more dramatic when utilities rose in price. In the nine instances of rising utility share prices, the stocks of the power companies that cut their dividends rose from 21% to 694% more than the index. The average outperformance was 178.7%.

A Tale of Two Decades

If these stocks didn't simply move with the utilities group on interest rate declines, why did they do better in the 1990s than in the 1980s? We believe that the market is viewing many electric utility dividend cuts in the current decade as aggressive and preemptive, while dividend reductions in the 1980s were seen as defensive and a reaction to events not under the power companies' control.

Much of the history of electric power in the 1980s was influenced by an event that occurred before the decade began. The accident at Three Mile Island in Pennsylvania in 1979 changed Americans' perception of nuclear power forever. Not a single new nuclear plant has been ordered in the U.S. since that accident. But before that incident, the U.S. electric power industry was enthusiastically building nuclear plants. Following the oil shocks of 1973 and 1979, electric utilities preferred to rely on nuclear energy rather than on imported oil to generate power. Consequently, a large number of nuclear plants were under construction when the Three Mile Island accident occurred. Some would be mothballed at great cost to the power companies that had begun to build them.

Many of the electric companies that cut their dividends in the 1980s did so because uncompleted nuclear plants had sapped their financial strength. Regulators were often unwilling to have the ratepayers bail out power companies that had made huge bets on nuclear plants. Instead, the shareholders paid by having their dividends cut.

The 1990s brought a new problem to the electric power industry: the threat of competition. Ever since Thomas Edison first wired lower Manhattan in the late 19th century, electric power has been considered a "natural monopoly." Generally, that meant it would be prohibitively expensive to set up two or more companies selling the same service in a particular territory. So, in place of competition, government regulators set the prices that customers would pay. But in recent years, other natural monopolies have fallen in the face of evidence that competition brings lower prices and better service. Long-distance and local phone service are now open to competition. Why not electric power?

A major step in the direction of open competition in the electric utility industry was the October 1992 passage of the National Energy Policy Act (NEPA). NEPA allowed federal regulators to authorize utilities to provide transmission service for any power generator (either another utility or an independent power company) to another electric utility. Although NEPA specifically prohibited authorizing transmission that would bypass the local utility to sell power to an end-user, most observers of the industry thought it would just be a matter of time before that was allowed, too.

Seven electric utilities cut their dividends between the passage of NEPA and the end of 1994. Four of the stocks were higher a year later, two were lower and one was essentially unchanged. On the surface, it looks as if we're back to a coin toss, since investors using a buy-on-the-cut strategy made money only 57% of the time.

But note some of the comments made by officials of these power companies when they cut their dividends. Three companies (Centerior Energy, TNP Enterprises, and New York State Electric & Gas) cited the likelihood of "increased competition." Although it did not specifically mention potential competition, FPL Group sounded a similar note, saying that a high dividend payout "takes away our financial flexibility." Edison International (then known as SCEcorp) cut its dividend by 30% two months after California regulators submitted a proposal that would allow every electricity consumer in the state to pick a power supplier by the year 2002. The company cited "uncertainty about the outlook" for future utility income.

In contrast, Central Maine Power and Sierra Pacific Resources made no mention of potential competition or the need to be more flexible. Central Maine cut its dividend 43% because regulators approved only part of the rate increase it sought. Sierra Pacific cut its dividend 39% because it needed to improve its capital position in light of a lower allowed rate of return. Shares of both Central Maine and Sierra Pacific were lower a year after they cut their dividends.

Of the five companies that appeared to be getting their financial houses in order to prepare for the future, only Centerior Energy saw its shares lower a year after the dividend cut. The other four (80% of the total) had higher share prices a year after they reduced their dividends. The average appreciation was 27.7%.

We should caution you that, while our study of electric utilities that cut their dividends to improve competitiveness strongly suggests that their stocks usually rise, our sample was very small. Since this is a rather new phenomenon, further studies will be needed to confirm our findings. We believe (and the evidence so far seems to confirm) that when electric utilities tell you they are reducing dividends to improve future results, it sends a strong signal that the market usually likes. Nevertheless, buying a stock on the news of a dividend cut remains an aggressive trading strategy. If you decide to attempt it, realize that you are taking a greater risk than you would in investing in a stock that steadily increases its dividend.

Summing Up

1. *Some utility stocks sport high yields because investors, fearing dividend cuts, avoid them.*

2. *Picking the highest-yielding utilities annually and holding them for a full year provided a greater total return than the market in a twenty-year simulation.*

3. *If a utility's dividend isn't cut, shareholders benefit from the higher yield. If it is, the share price often rebounds quickly.*

4. *In recent years, shares of electric utilities that cut dividends to prepare for increasing competition usually were higher in price a year later.*

9
Selected Stocks Worth Buying

By now, we hope you are convinced that our strategy of buying quality stocks that have good dividend records is a solid way to invest for the long term. So far in this book, we've given you lists of hundreds of stocks that fit various dividend criteria. Some readers will consider these lists as raw materials for a creative search to find the stocks that best suit their needs. Others may just find the sheer number of interesting stocks overwhelming.

If you're in the second group, the twenty-four thumbnail sketches of stocks that follow may help you narrow the field. We've divided them into four separate groups of six stocks each. Some equities clearly fit into more than one category. We made the final selection in each group with an eye toward industry diversification.

Although we find these stocks attractive for the long haul, don't simply take our word for it. Check out recent developments in each company either through a recognized research service (see Appendix A for some sources) or by reading the company's latest SEC filings. We've included addresses and phone numbers for each company so that you can follow up on your own.

While we've included historical data on dividend growth and total return through the end of 1995, we deliberately left out valuation measures such as P/E ratio (price-earnings, or how much you are paying for each dollar of expected company earnings) and current yield. Since these measures depend on a stock's price on any given day, we've left it up to you to decide if the stocks are attractive for purchase when you read this book.

We've included a chart of each stock's monthly price action for the three years ended 1995. Note that some of these stocks have split since these charts were created.

For comparison, the benchmark S&P 500 index posted an annualized total return of 11.8% for the ten years ended December 31, 1995.

Group I: Stocks You Can Buy Directly

The following suggested stocks are for younger investors who are employed and don't depend on dividend income to meet living expenses. Each of the companies profiled permits you to bypass a broker and to buy shares directly, if you join its dividend reinvestment plan. Each also permits regular optional cash payments. As we saw in Chap. 5, DRPs are a convenient, inexpensive way to build a portfolio.

The six stocks make up a diverse group, with representation in insurance, oil, restaurants, consumer products, banking, and food. We believe they have above-average earnings and dividend growth prospects.

AFLAC

1932 Wynnton Rd.
Columbus, GA 31999
(706) 323-3431

AFL/New York Stock Exchange
Dividends paid since 1973
S&P earnings and dividend ranking: A
Indicated annual dividend as of December 31, 1995: $0.52
Increase in dividends from 1991 to 1995: 71%
$1,000 invested on 12/31/1985 worth on 12/31/1995 with
dividends reinvested: $6,080
Ten-year annualized total return: 19.8%

AFLAC, a holding company with insurance and broad-casting interests, derived 85% of its revenues from Japan in 1995. The company is the dominant underwriter of supplemental cancer insurance in Japan and has capital-ized on that strength, as well as on its low-cost producer status, to exploit new market and product niches. In the U.S., a product expansion program away from cancer cov-erage and toward higher margin products, combined with stepped-up marketing efforts, bodes well for long-term premium growth. AFLAC owns seven network-affiliated television stations, primarily located in the southwestern U.S. Earnings over the five years through 1995 have grown at an average annual rate of 25%. The dividend, al-though only $0.52 annually, is up more than threefold since 1986.

DIVIDEND REINVESTMENT PLAN DETAILS

$750 investment to join plan.

Optional cash payments of $50 per investment to $120,000 annually may be made. The payments are invested twice monthly, around the 1st and 15th.

Automatic withdrawal from checking accounts is available.

Figure 9-1. AFLAC Inc. (AFL)

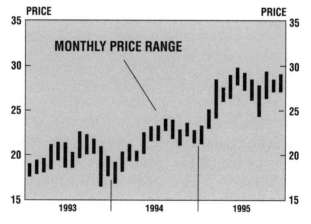

McDonald's Corp.

Campus Office Bldg.
Kroc Drive
Oakbrook, IL 60521
(708) 575-3000

MCD/New York Stock Exchange
Dividends paid since 1976
S&P earnings and dividend ranking: A+
Indicated annual dividend as of December 31, 1995: $0.27
Increase in dividends from 1991 to 1995: 45%
$1,000 invested on 12/31/1985 worth on 12/31/1995 with
dividends reinvested: $5,508
Ten-year annualized total return: 18.6%

One of the most recognized global brand names, McDonald's is the largest fast-food restaurant company in the U.S. and in the world. At the end of 1995, about 38% of its more than 15,000 restaurants were outside the U.S. Earnings, which have risen at an annual rate of 12% over the past five years, should continue to increase at a double-digit rate, paced by international operations.

In recent years, foreign operations have accounted for more than 50% of total profits. Operating earnings from international restaurants should increase faster than domestic profits. In foreign markets, additional benefits from economies of scale are likely as the company's presence continues to grow.

The company has a large, ongoing share-repurchase program. Dividends, although modest, have jumped 145% since 1986.

DIVIDEND REINVESTMENT PLAN DETAILS

$1,000, or $100 per month via an automatic withdrawal plan from checking or savings accounts, to join plan. For prospectus and enrollment form, contact company at 1-800-228-9623.

Optional cash payments of $100 per investment to $250,000 annually may be made. The payments are invested weekly.

Fees: enrollment fee, $5; annual account fee, $3; $1 per share trading fee, capped at $5 per trade; $1 for automatic investment.

Figure 9-2. McDonald's Corp. (MCD)

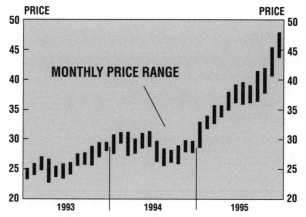

Mobil Corp.

3225 Gallows Rd.
Fairfax, VA 22037
(703) 846-3000

MOB/New York Stock Exchange
Dividends paid since 1902
S&P earnings and dividend ranking: B+
Indicated annual dividend as of December 31, 1995: $3.70
Increase in dividends from 1991 to 1995: 16%
$1,000 invested on 12/31/1985 worth on 12/31/1995 with
dividends reinvested: $5,806
Ten-year annualized total return: 19.2%

Mobil, a global integrated petroleum company and a leading chemicals maker, maintains an aggressive exploration program. It has some 20,000 retail gasoline outlets in high growth markets. With recent cost-cutting moves, the company is among the best positioned of the major oil producers from a cost/efficiency standpoint. A strong presence in the growing Pacific Rim markets should continue to aid profitability in the years ahead. A healthy balance sheet and cash generating capacity should support expansion of international exploration, as well as future dividend hikes. Since Mobil's products are based on a volatile commodity, much of which comes from areas of the world that have had some instability, outside forces can have a significant effect on the stock price.

DIVIDEND REINVESTMENT PLAN DETAILS

$250 minimum investment to join plan. For prospectus and enrollment form, contact Chemical Mellon Shareholder Services at 1-800-648-9291.

Optional cash payments of $50 to $7,500 monthly may be made. The payments are invested on the 10th and 25th of each month.

You may open an Individual Retirement Account (IRA) via Mobil's DRP.

Figure 9-3. Mobil Corp. (MOB)

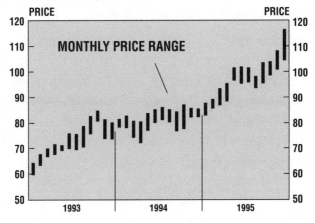

Procter & Gamble

1 Procter & Gamble Plaza
Cincinnati, OH 45202
(800) 742-6253

PG/New York Stock Exchange
Dividends paid since 1891
S&P earnings and dividend ranking: A
Indicated annual dividend as of December 31, 1995: $1.60
Increase in dividends from 1991 to 1995: 50%
$1,000 invested on 12/31/1985 worth on 12/31/1995 with
dividends reinvested: $6,065
Ten-year annualized total return: 19.8%

Procter & Gamble is a leading consumer products company operating in more than 140 countries. Familiar brand names include Tide, Cascade, Dawn, Downy, Max Factor, Secret, Safeguard, Folgers, Jif, Duncan Hines, Crisco, Bounty, Charmin, and Pampers. P&G also makes drugs for the treatment of ulcers and bone and heart problems.

The company's earnings over the years have grown steadily, and Standard & Poor's expects profits to climb 12% to 14% annually for the next few years, fueled by new household and personal products and further penetration of emerging growth markets. Dividends, which have been increased for forty consecutive years (as of 1995) should also remain in an uptrend.

Long-term results should be enhanced by increasing use of Olean (Olestra), a calorie-free fat replacement food product that was approved for use in snack foods by the FDA in early 1996.

DIVIDEND REINVESTMENT PLAN DETAILS

$100 minimum investment to join plan. For prospectus and enrollment form, contact J.P. Morgan/P&G at 1-800-742-6253

Optional cash payments of $100 monthly to $120,000 annually may be made. The payments are invested twice a month.

Automatic withdrawal from checking accounts is available.

Fee: 5% of investment ($1 maximum).

Figure 9-4. Procter & Gamble (PG)

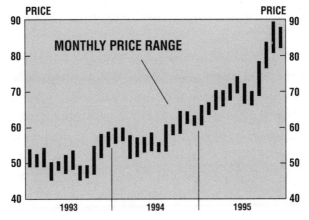

Regions Financial

417 North 20th St.
Birmingham AL 35202
(205) 326-7100

RGBK/Nasdaq
Dividends paid since 1968
S&P earnings and dividend ranking: A+
Indicated annual dividend as of December 31, 1995: $1.40
Increase in dividends from 1991 to 1995: 49%
$1,000 invested on 12/31/1985 worth on 12/31/1995 with
dividends reinvested: $4,268
Ten-year annualized total return: 15.6%

Formerly First Alabama Bancshares, Regions Financial is a major southeastern bank holding company operating more than 280 offices in Alabama, Florida, Georgia, Louisiana, and Tennessee. This service territory is seeing growth higher than the national average.

The bank's asset quality is well above that of its peers. Regions has traditionally taken a conservative approach to loan-loss provisions. At the end of 1995, reserves for loan losses amounted to 1.36% of net loans outstanding. Net chargeoffs in 1995 were only 0.13% of average loans outstanding.

Earnings have increased at an average annual rate of 15% over the past five years. Dividends have surged 141% in the decade since 1986. Future earnings should be fueled by growth in non-interest income (various customer fees) and by a continued aggressive acquisition program. The bank made nine acquisitions in 1994 and four in 1995.

DIVIDEND REINVESTMENT PLAN DETAILS

$500 minimum investment to join plan. For prospectus and enrollment form, contact First Chicago Trust at 1-800-446-2617

Optional cash payments of $100 to $10,000 monthly may be made. The payments are invested once a month.

Automatic withdrawal from checking or savings accounts is available.

Figure 9-5. Regions Financial (RGBK)

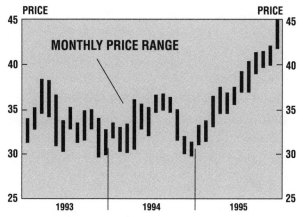

Tyson Foods

2210 W. Oaklawn Dr.
Springdale, AR 72762
(501) 290-4000

TYSNA/Nasdaq
Dividends paid since 1976
S&P earnings and dividend ranking: A+
Indicated annual dividend as of December 31, 1995: $0.12
Increase in dividends from 1991 to 1995: 157%
$1,000 invested on 12/31/1985 worth on 12/31/1995 with
dividends reinvested: $5,830
Ten-year annualized total return: 19.3%

The world's largest producer, processor, and marketer of poultry-based food products, Tyson sells 55% of its output through food service channels and 45% retail. Value-enhanced products include chicken patties and nuggets and precooked chicken. Basic poultry items include chilled and prepackaged fresh chicken. The company's products are sold under the Tyson, Holly Farms, and Weaver names.

Continued consolidation of the U.S. chicken processing industry and growing global chicken consumption should lift per-share earnings of this low-risk stock over the next few years. Tyson's decision to put its troubled beef and pork processing operations up for sale should sharpen the company's focus on profit growth.

DIVIDEND REINVESTMENT PLAN DETAILS

$250 minimum investment to join plan. For prospectus and enrollment form, contact First Chicago Trust at 1-800-822-7096

Optional cash payments of at least $50 ($25 if via automatic withdrawal) may be made. There is no maximum. The payments are invested once a week. Fees: $7.50 plus about $0.03 a share for initial transaction only. No purchase fees for subsequent investment. Automatic withdrawal from checking or savings accounts is available ($1 fee per withdrawal).

Figure 9-6. Tyson Foods (TYSNA)

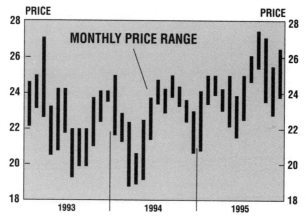

Group II: Stocks with Outstanding Dividend Growth

The six stocks that follow, all taken from Table 3-2, have outstanding records of dividend growth. Each has increased its payments to shareholders by at least 400% over the last decade. Investors should consider these issues as excellent long-term holdings. Even if you are close to or in retirement, your portfolio generally should contain companies that rapidly increase their dividend payments. Over time, you will be better off than if you buy companies that have high current yield but provide little in the way of dividend growth. As we saw in Chap. 3, stocks with strong dividend growth can offset the effects of inflation.

Cooper Tire & Rubber

Lima & Western Avenues
Findlay, OH 45840
(419) 423-1321

CTB/New York Stock Exchange
Dividends paid since 1950
S&P earnings and dividend ranking: A
Indicated annual dividend as of December 31, 1995: $0.30
Increase in dividends from 1991 to 1995: 108%
$1,000 invested on 12/31/85 worth on 12/31/95 with
dividends reinvested: $11,283
Ten-year annualized total return: 27.4%

Cooper is the fourth largest tire manufacturer in the U.S. and the ninth largest worldwide. Other rubber products include inner tubes, vibration control products, hoses and hose assemblies, automotive body and window sealing systems, and specialty seating component. The company's tires are sold exclusively in the replacement market through Sears, Pep Boys, and some 2,000 independent dealers and distributors. Tires are sold under the Cooper, Falls Mastercraft, and Starfire brands as well as under private label names. In recent years, the independent dealer market accounted for about two-thirds of all replacement passenger vehicle tires sold in the U.S.

Although Cooper's 1995 earnings were lower than its 1994 results due to higher raw materials costs, the company continued to gain market share. Despite a decline in total replacement tire sales in 1995, Cooper's unit sales were at an all-time high.

The company should benefit from favorable trends, including a growing vehicle population and a continued increase in miles driven per vehicle. We expect Cooper's earnings to get back on track. Dividends, up 500% in the past decade, should continue to rise.

Figure 9-7. Cooper Tire & Rubber (CTB)

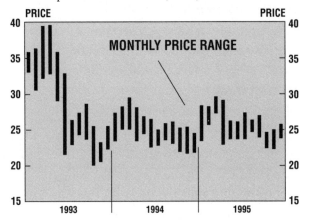

CORUS Bankshares

Lincoln National Bank Building
3959 North Lincoln Avenue
Chicago, IL 60613
(312) 549-7100

CORS/Nasdaq
Dividends paid since 1971
S&P earnings and dividend ranking: A
Indicated annual dividend as of December 31, 1995: $0.40
Increase in dividends from 1991 to 1995: 118%
$1,000 invested on 12/31/85 worth on 12/31/95 with
dividends reinvested: $6,530
Ten-year annualized total return: 20.6%

Chances are you've never heard of CORUS Bankshares, even under its previous name, River Forest Bancorp. Most people on Wall Street never did either. Only three securities analysts follow this small ($2 billion in assets) Chicago-based bank holding company. In contrast, twenty-five analysts have earnings estimates on the company's cross-town neighbor, the giant ($122 billion in assets) First Chicago NBD. In 1995, CORUS split its stock 2-for-1 and increased its dividend 14%. That represented the eighth split since 1967 and twenty years of increasing dividends. As we saw in Table 3-2, had you bought CORUS shares in 1985, the indicated dividend in 1995 would have provided a yield on original investment of 10.8%. Over that decade, CORUS raised its cash payments to shareholders by 1,233%. The company has made several strategic acquisitions and shows great entrepreneurial spirit.

For example, in January 1994, CORUS purchased $150 million in nonperforming student loans for $13.5 million. By the end of 1995, it had turned $48 million worth of these loans into good credits. We expect CORUS to continue to post strong earnings and dividend increases. Ultimately, as the banking industry consolidates, the company could be acquired. It would have to be a friendly merger, however, since insiders control 50% of the stock.

Figure 9-8. CORUS Bankshares (CORS)

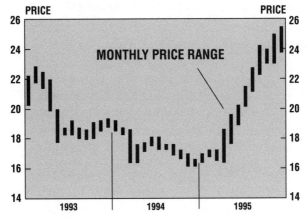

Loctite Corp.

10 Columbus Blvd.
Hartford CT 06106
(860) 520-5000

LOC/New York Stock Exchange
Dividends paid since 1962
S&P earnings and dividend ranking: A
Indicated annual dividend as of December 31, 1995: $1.00
Increase in dividends from 1991 to 1995: 39%
$1,000 invested on 12/31/85 worth on 12/31/95 with
dividends reinvested: $6,697
Ten-year annualized total return: 20.9%
A dividend reinvestment plan is available.

Loctite manufactures and sells adhesives, sealants, coatings, and specialty chemicals for industrial and consumer applications. Industrial users account for about 56% of the company's sales, while consumer products are 27% and the auto aftermarket is 17%. Product lines include thread locking sealants, structural adhesives, instant adhesives, gasketing compounds, automotive body repair materials, home care products, sealants for electronic components, lubricating and cleaning compounds, and other specialty chemicals. Although 1995 per-share earnings were relatively flat because of a restructuring charge and weakness in North American industrial and automotive markets, the company has favorable long-term growth prospects. More than half of Loctite's sales are outside North America and this geographic segment should grow rapidly. In addition, the company's new consumer products, a reformulated super glue and a glue that sets in the microwave, show great promise. Stock performance should get a boost from the repurchase of up to 3.35 million common shares (9.5% of those outstanding), authorized by directors in October 1995. The company's dividend, increased some 400% in the decade ending 1995, should continue to grow.

Figure 9-9. Loctite Corp. (LOC)

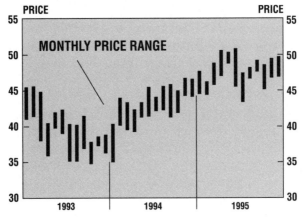

Merck & Co.

One Merck Drive
P.O. Box 100
Whitehorse Station, NJ 08889
(908) 423-1000

MRK/New York Stock Exchange
Dividends paid since 1935
S&P earnings and dividend ranking: A+
Indicated annual dividend as of December 31, 1995: $1.36
Increase in dividends from 1991 to 1995: 61%
$1,000 invested on 12/31/85 worth on 12/31/95 with
dividends reinvested: $10,605
Ten-year annualized total return: 26.6%
A dividend reinvestment plan is available.

One of the world's premier pharmaceutical research companies (R&D was almost 8% of 1995 revenues), Merck has concentrated its efforts on creating breakthrough drugs to treat chronic illnesses. Recent additions to its drug lineup include Fosamax for treatment of osteoporosis and Crixivan, a protease inhibitor for AIDS. Each could become a major product for the company in the years ahead. Cardiovascular drugs (about 36% of sales) are an important category for Merck. Its cholesterol-lowering agents, Mevacor and Zocor, control about 40% of the worldwide market. In addition, Merck is a leading player in managed care through its Medco unit, which manages pharmacy benefits for some 47 million Americans.

As Merck's research thrived, so did its shareholders. Had you purchased Merck shares at their average price in

1985, your dividend a decade later would have provided a 21.5% yield on your original investment. We expect Merck to continue to do well. Although politicians like to criticize drug companies for the cost of their medications, often drug therapy is significantly less expensive than alternatives. Furthermore, Merck's Medco unit, acquired in November 1993, enables the company to profit from health care cost-containment efforts.

Figure 9-10. Merck & Co. (MRK)

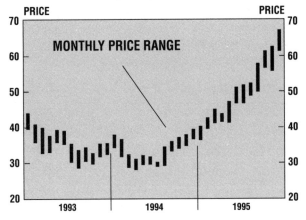

PepsiCo, Inc.

700 Anderson Hill Rd.
Purchase, NY 10577
(914) 253-2000

PEP/New York Stock Exchange
Dividends paid since 1952
S&P earnings and dividend ranking: A+
Indicated annual dividend as of December 31, 1995: $0.80
Increase in dividends from 1991 to 1995: 73%
$1,000 invested on 12/31/85 worth on 12/31/95 with
dividends reinvested: $8,126
Ten-year annualized total return: 23.3%
A dividend reinvestment plan is available.

You may think of PepsiCo as a beverage company. It is, and some 37% of its profits come from Pepsi-Cola, Mountain Dew, Slice, Mug, and other soda brands. (Outside the U.S., the company also has the rights to the 7Up brand.) But PEP sells far more than soda. Its Frito-Lay unit (41% of 1995 profits) produces the best-selling line of snack foods in the U.S. Brands include Fritos, Lay's, Ruffles, Doritos, and Chee-tos. Frito-Lay has a dominant position (a market share of more than 50%) in the $15 billion salty snack business.

In addition, PepsiCo is one of the world's largest restaurant companies (22% of profits) with its Pizza Hut, Taco Bell, and KFC (formerly Kentucky Fried Chicken) fast-food chains. The company recently shifted its restaurant emphasis to franchising and away from the more capital-intensive ownership of units. The savings will be

plowed back into the beverage and snack foods businesses, which provide higher returns.

International operations now account for less than a
third of sales and should grow rapidly in the years ahead.
Through the end of 1995, PepsiCo had raised its dividend for 24 consecutive years. We expect the increases to
continue.

Figure 9-11. PepsiCo, Inc. (PEP)

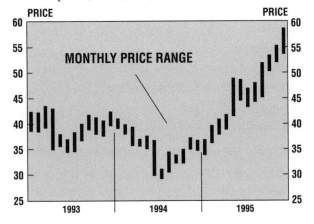

Sysco Corp.

1390 Enclave Parkway
Houston, TX 77077
(713) 584-1390

SYY/New York Stock Exchange
Dividends paid since 1970
S&P earnings and dividend ranking: A+
Indicated annual dividend as of December 31, 1995: $0.52
Increase in dividends from 1991 to 1995: 214%
$1,000 invested on 12/31/85 worth on 12/31/95 with
dividends reinvested: $6,357
Ten-year annualized total return: 20.3%

This company is the giant of the U.S. food service distribution industry, selling products to more than 255,000
customers in the "dining-out" industry. Sysco sells a full
line of fresh, frozen, canned, and dry foods to restaurants,
cafeterias, and other out-of-home food servers. In addition to foods, the company distributes paper products,
tableware, kitchen equipment, and cleaning supplies.
Products include both national brands and goods packed
under Sysco's private label. The company's broader line
of product offerings includes such items as fresh meats,
imported specialties, and fresh produce.

Although it is the food service distribution industry
leader, Sysco still has room to grow; it controls only about
10% of the highly-fragmented $130 billion industry.
About 60% of the company's customers are restaurants,
while hospitals and nursing homes are another 12%.

We expect the domestic food service industry to continue growing at about 3% a year as Americans, always pressed for time, take more of their meals away from home. Sysco's per-share earnings growth should be 12% to 15% annually over the next few years as the company gains market share at the expense of its weaker rivals. Dividends, up 940% in the decade ending 1995, should increase regularly.

Figure 9-12. Sysco Corp. (SYY)

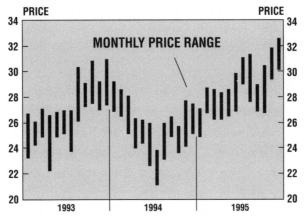

Group III: Top Quality Stocks

The following is a suggested portfolio for more conservative investors. All six of the stocks carry Standard & Poor's highest earnings and dividend ranking of A+, indicating at least a decade of superior earnings and dividend growth and stability.

The letter rankings (commonly called "quality rankings") are historical and are not intended to predict stock price movement. By their nature, however, many issues ranked A+ have low volatility and hold out the promise of good long-term performance. Therefore, the issues are generally suitable for conservative investors with a longer time horizon.

Albertson's

250 Parkcenter Blvd.
P.O. Box 20
Boise, ID 83726
(208) 385-6200

ABS/New York Stock Exchange
Dividends paid since 1960
Indicated annual dividend as of December 31, 1995: $0.52.
Increase in dividends from 1985 to 1995: 462%
$1,000 invested on 12/31/1985 worth on 12/31/1995 with
dividends reinvested: $9,363
Ten-year annualized total return: 25%
A dividend reinvestment plan is available.

The fourth largest food retailer in the U.S., Albertson's operates more than 725 supermarkets and combination food-drug stores in nineteen states. Although food retailing has rather low margins, it is a high-volume business. The company attempts to increase sales volume in its stores by focusing on "quick meal ideas" and non-grocery services, which include pharmacies and in-store banks. At the end of fiscal 1996 (January), there were 54 in-store banks and 481 in-store pharmacies.

Albertson's earnings gains over the past ten years have averaged 18%. Retail operations are supported by eleven company-owned distribution centers. Strong management and a presence in areas with expanding populations bode well for future profit growth. Healthy cash flow provides ample funds for an ongoing share-repurchase program and a $3.4 billion capital spending plan for the five years from 1995 through 1999. The plan includes building 351 new stores and making 242 remodels.

Over the next few years, Albertson's management aims for a 12% return on average assets and a 15% annual gain in per-share earnings. The company has repurchased fifteen million shares in recent years and directors have adopted a program to repurchase up to seven million more.

Figure 9-13. Albertson's (ABS)

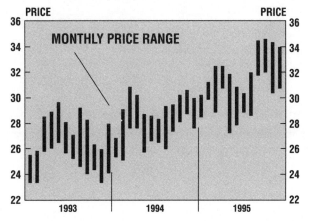

Coca-Cola Co.

1 Coca-Cola Plaza N.W.
Atlanta, GA 30313
(404) 676-2121

KO/New York Stock Exchange
Dividends paid since 1893
Indicated annual dividend as of December 31, 1995: $0.88
Increase in dividends from 1985 to 1995: 257%
$1,000 invested on 12/31/1985 worth on 12/31/1995 with
dividends reinvested: $12,680
Ten-year annualized total return: 29%
A dividend reinvestment plan is available.

Coca-Cola, the world's largest soft drink producer, is the most recognized brand name in the world. A major factor behind the company's solid earnings and dividend record has been its aggressive pursuit of less-developed markets around the world. Coke does business in 195 countries, deriving nearly 70% of total revenues and 80% of operating profits from regions outside the more mature U.S. market. That gives the company substantial insulation from the inevitable economic downturns of any one region.

In addition, with per-capita consumption of soft drink products outside the U.S. at only 11% of the U.S. level, there is strong growth potential. Coca-Cola's huge infrastructure gives it the resources and competitive advantage to realize this potential. The company has equity positions in more than 30 unconsolidated bottling and distribution operations, including bottlers representing about 43% of the company's U.S. case volume in 1995.

Standard & Poor's expects Coca-Cola's rapid earnings growth, high return on invested capital, dependable dividend growth, and strong balance sheet to continue to make the stock an attractive portfolio holding.

Figure 9-14. Coca-Cola Co. (KO)

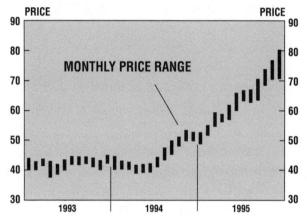

Gillette Co.

Prudential Tower Bldg.
Boston, MA 02199
(617) 421-7000

G/New York Stock Exchange
Dividends paid since 1906
Indicated annual dividend as of December 31, 1995: $0.60
Increase in dividends from 1985 to 1995: 269%
$1,000 invested on 12/31/1985 worth on 12/31/1995 with
dividends reinvested: $14,288
Ten-year annualized total return: 30%
A dividend reinvestment plan is available.

This well-known global maker of razors and blades, hair care products, toiletries, writing instruments, and small appliances has recorded strong earnings growth, a high return on equity and an impressive return on sales over the years. Popular brand names include Braun, Right Guard, White Rain, Silkience, Parker Pen, Papermate, and Oral-B. Gillette enjoys leading positions in nearly all of its markets.

Profit margins of the company's largest business, blades and razors, continue to widen on higher volume and a better mix. The greatest volume growth is occurring in international markets, as the company expands its presence in untapped regions, especially in Asia and Latin America.

As we were about to go to press, Gillette announced the acquisition of Duracell, the world's leading maker of alkaline batteries for about $7 billion worth of Gillette stock. The move makes batteries the second largest business segment for the company and adds an important product line that Gillette can sell, especially in Europe and in emerging growth markets where it already has a major presence.

Figure 9-15. Gillette Co. (G)

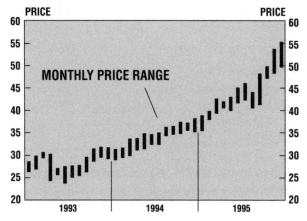

International Flavors & Fragrances

521 W. 57th St.
New York, NY 10019
(212) 765-5500

IFF/New York Stock Exchange
Dividends paid since 1956
Indicated annual dividend as of December 31, 1995: $1.36
Increase in dividends from 1985 to 1995: 264%
$1,000 invested on 12/31/1985 worth on 12/31/1995 with
dividends reinvested: $4,713
Ten-year annualized total return: 16.8%
A dividend reinvestment plan is available.

IFF is a leading maker of products used by other manu-facturers to impart or improve flavor or fragrance in a wide variety of consumer goods. Flavor products are sold main-ly to food and beverage companies for use in such con-sumer products as soft drinks, candies, cake mixes, desserts, and alcoholic beverages. The increased market for low calorie and low fat foods enhances the demand for flavor products. Flavors are also used in pharmaceuticals. IFF's fragrances are used in soaps, detergents, cosmetics, and air fresheners.

We expect the company to extend its healthy profit growth in the years ahead. Two-thirds of IFF's revenues and earnings are generated from outside the U.S., with the Far East, Latin America, and Eastern Europe the most promising growth markets as standards of living rapidly improve and demand for higher quality consumer products increases.

The dividend has been raised each year for the past thirty-five. The company has virtually no debt, which will allow it to continue to boost capital spending while repurchasing shares.

Figure 9-16. International Flavors & Fragrances (IFF)

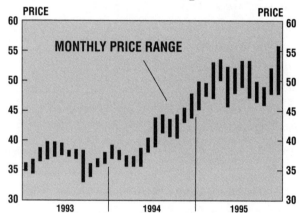

Johnson & Johnson

One Johnson & Johnson Plaza
New Brunswick, NJ 08933
(908) 524-0400

JNJ/New York Stock Exchange
Dividends paid since 1905
Indicated annual dividend as of December 31, 1995: 1.32
Increase in dividends from 1985 to 1995: 314%
$1,000 invested on 12/31/1985 worth on 12/31/1995 with
dividends reinvested: $7,859
Ten-year annualized total return: 22.9%
A dividend reinvestment plan is available.

The world's largest health care company's commanding positions in rapidly expanding medical markets point to continued strong earnings growth for the foreseeable future.

Best-selling pharmaceuticals include Ortho-Novum oral contraceptives, Propulsid gastrointestinal, Sporanox antifungal, and Retin-A for acne. A form of the latter (Renova) came on the market in early 1996 for reduction of facial wrinkles, brown spots, and surface roughness. Renova should chalk up sales of several hundred million dollars annually.

J&J's medical devices business should benefit from continued strong demand for its coronary stent and the 1996 acquisition of Cordis, a leader in angiography and angioplasty.

Johnson & Johnson has unmatched product diversity and geographic reach. Foreign operations accounted for

51% of sales and 48% of profits in 1995. The company's consumer products include Johnson's baby powder, Tylenol analgesic, Band-Aid adhesive bandages, Reach toothbrushes, and Neutrogena skin care products.

Figure 9-17. Johnson & Johnson (JNJ)

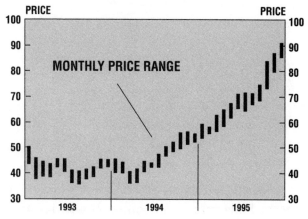

Wilmington Trust

Rodney Sq. North
Wilmington, DE 19890
(302) 651-1000

WILM/Nasdaq
Dividends paid since 1914
Indicated annual dividend as of December 31, 1995: $1.20
Increase in dividends from 1985 to 1995: 336%
$1,000 invested on 12/31/1985 worth on 12/31/1995 with
dividends reinvested: $4,542
Ten-year annualized total return: 16.3%
A dividend reinvestment plan is available.

This bank holding company, through its Wilmington Trust Co. subsidiary, operates more than sixty branches offering a broad variety of financial services, mainly in Wilmington, Delaware. The company also has offices in Maryland, Pennsylvania, and Florida. Gross loans outstanding were $3.53 billion at the end of 1995, up from $3.29 billion a year earlier. Commercial, financial, and agricultural loans were 33% of the total, commercial mortgages 22%, and residential mortgages 19%. At the end of 1995, the company's reserve for loan losses was 1.47% of average loans, while net chargeoffs during the year were 0.23% of average loans.

Earnings have grown at an annual rate of 6% over the past five years, while dividends have increased at a 12% rate. Profits should continue to grow, as the bank expands, particularly in Florida, and as fee income rises. High asset quality and strong management are major pluses.

Figure 9-18. Wilmington Trust (WILM)

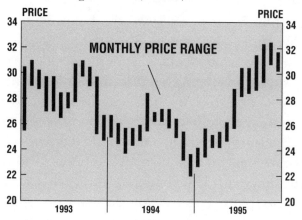

Group IV: Higher-Yielding Stocks for Current Income

As we write this in early 1996, the following six stocks have dividend yields at least twice the 2.2% yield of the S&P 500. Investors seeking current income may find these issues attractive. Often that means retired individuals who count on stock dividends to pay some of their living costs. As people live longer, the number of years the average person spends in retirement increases. Consequently, we believe that even retired people will do better over time with lower-yielding stocks that raise their dividends rapidly. Even if you do need investment income for regular expenses, add some low-yielding, growing-dividend stocks (see Group II) to your portfolio mix.

American Brands

1700 East Putnam Ave.
Old Greenwich, CT 06870
(203) 698-5000

AMB/New York Stock Exchange
Dividends paid since 1905
S&P earnings and dividend ranking: A−
Indicated annual dividend as of December 31, 1995: $2.00
Increase in dividends from 1985 to 1995: 26%
$1,000 invested on 12/31/1985 worth on 12/31/1995 with
dividends reinvested: $4,136
Ten-year annualized total return: 15.3%
A dividend reinvestment plan is available.

Since shedding its American Tobacco Co. (and any potential liability from that business) in 1994, AMB's only exposure to the tobacco industry is its ownership of U.K.-based Gallaher Ltd. Gallaher controls 39% of the British cigarette market with brands that include Benson & Hedges, Silk Cut, and Berkeley. American Brands also produces distilled spirits (Jim Beam, Old Grand-Dad, Gilbeys, and DeKuyper), hardware and home improvement products (Moen, Master Lock, and Aristokraft), office products (Swingline and ACCO World), and golf products (Titleist, Acushnet, and Cobra). The company's strong portfolio of relatively recession-resistant businesses generates high cash flow; both tobacco and liquor operations have low capital requirements. The cash is likely to be used to maintain the current high dividend, reduce debt, and buy back shares. We expect the elimination of

U.S. tobacco uncertainties to smooth the company's future earnings growth stream. At the same time, AMB is likely to make add-on acquisitions to bolster its existing operations.

Figure 9-19. American Brands (AMB)

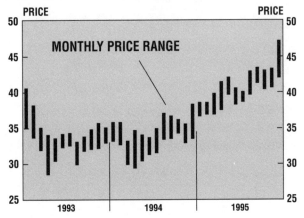

Central & South West

1616 Woodall Rodgers Freeway
Dallas, TX 75202
(214) 777-1000

CSR/New York Stock Exchange
Dividends paid since 1947
S&P earnings and dividend ranking: A−
Indicated annual dividend as of December 31, 1995: $1.72
Increase in dividends from 1985 to 1995: 18%
$1,000 invested on 12/31/1985 worth on 12/31/1995 with
dividends reinvested: $3,771
Ten-year annualized total return: 14.2%
A dividend reinvestment plan is available.

Through its subsidiaries, this electric utility holding company provides electric and gas service to 1.6 million customers in Texas, Oklahoma, Louisiana, and Arkansas. The company recently acquired SEEBOARD, plc, a highly efficient U.K. electric utility. SEEBOARD serves some two million customers in an affluent suburban and rural area of southeastern England. The service area has above-average economic growth. SEEBOARD is also involved in gas supply, electrical contracting, and retailing.

Central & South West's long-term prospects are enhanced by growth in demand in its service territory, an extensive transmission system, and strong non-utility businesses. CSR's nonregulated operations include CSW Energy, a developer of cogeneration projects; CSW Credit, which buys electric utilities' accounts receivable; and EnerShop, a cost-control consulting subsidiary.

The company's balance sheet is strong, with long-term debt approximately 53% of total capitalization. Dividends, which through the end of 1995 had been increased for forty-five consecutive years, should continue to grow modestly.

Figure 9-20. Central & South West (CSR)

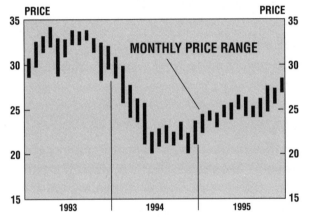

Meditrust

197 First Ave.
Needham Heights, MA 02194
(617) 433-6000

MT/New York Stock Exchange
Dividends paid since 1986
S&P earnings and dividend ranking: NR
Indicated annual dividend as of December 31, 1995: $2.70
Increase in dividends from 1985 to 1995: 13%
$1,000 invested on 12/31/1985 worth on 12/31/1995 with
dividends reinvested: $6,351
Ten-year annualized total return: 20.3%
A dividend reinvestment plan is available.

Meditrust is the nation's largest health care real estate investment trust (REIT). The trust owns (and leases to operators) or holds mortgages on a growing portfolio of nursing homes, rehabilitation facilities, and other medical properties. The company has an excellent record of earnings and dividend growth. Through the end of 1995, MT had raised its dividend in every quarter since it began paying dividends in 1986. The company does not receive an S&P earnings and dividend rank because the system does not evaluate REITs.

The aging U.S. population bodes well for the continued growth of the nursing home business. Although potential reductions in the growth of Medicare and Medicaid spending could have an adverse effect on profits of nursing home operators that lease from MT, the company is partially insulated because real estate-related costs typically are a small part of a nursing home's total budget.

Meditrust plans to expand its property base by financing assisted living centers. These facilities offer lifestyle amenities to people who do not require full-time nursing home care.

Figure 9-21. Meditrust (MT)

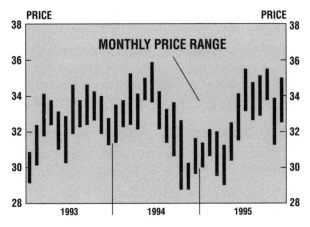

Peoples Energy Corp.

130 E. Randolph Dr.
Chicago, IL 60601
(312) 240-4000

PGL/New York Stock Exchange
Dividends paid since 1937
S&P earnings and dividend ranking: B+
Indicated annual dividend as of December 31, 1995: $1.80
Increase in dividends from 1985 to 1995: 6%
$1,000 invested on 12/31/1985 worth on 12/31/1995 with
dividends reinvested: $3,071
Ten-year annualized total return: 11.9%
A dividend reinvestment plan is available.

This holding company serves 972,000 customers through two gas utilities in Chicago and northeastern Illinois. Some 73% of revenues are from residential accounts. Although residential space heating is likely to remain PGL's largest market, long-term growth will be tied to development of the gas air conditioning, cogeneration, and natural gas vehicle markets. The company's proximity to several major interstate pipeline systems gives it a very low cost of gas, enabling Peoples to compete effectively with alternate fuel sources.

Through a subsidiary, the company is a 50% participant in a partnership formed to provide heating and cooling services (under a 28-year contract) to the McCormick Place exposition and convention center and other large buildings in Chicago.

In late 1994, the company's utility subsidiaries began a major project to re-engineer their operations in an effort to increase efficiency and cost-effectiveness. Recent reductions in the size of the company's work force are contributing to productivity gains. Although the company paid out 101% of its earnings in fiscal 1995 (ended September), rate relief will boost 1996 profits, while cash flow should remain healthy.

Figure 9-22. Peoples Energy Corp. (PGL)

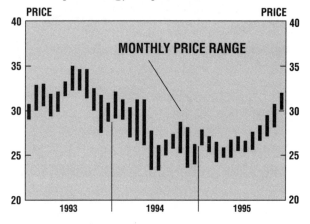

SCANA Corp.

1426 Main Street
Columbia, SC 29201
(803) 748-3000

SCG/New York Stock Exchange
Dividends paid since 1946
S&P earnings and dividend ranking: A–
Indicated annual dividend as of December 31, 1995: $1.44
Increase in dividends from 1985 to 1995: 10%
$1,000 invested on 12/31/1985 worth on 12/31/1995 with
dividends reinvested: $3,861
Ten-year annualized total return: 14.5%
A dividend reinvestment plan is available.

This holding company for South Carolina Electric & Gas (SCE&G) also provides bus service in metropolitan areas of Columbia and Charleston. Nonregulated subsidiaries are engaged in natural gas exploration and production, gas marketing, propane storage and distribution, power plant management and maintenance, and wireless personal telecommunications services.

SCE&G serves 484,000 electric customers and 243,000 natural gas customers in central, southern, and southwestern South Carolina. Residential sales of electricity accounted for 32% of SCANA's 1995 kilowatt hour (KWH) sales; commercial and industrial sales were each 29% of the company's total.

SCE&G's cost-containment efforts have been successful and the utility is one of the lowest-cost producers in its region. About 64% of the company's fuel mix is coal, 27% nuclear, and 4% hydro.

Through 1995, SCANA had paid higher dividends for twenty consecutive years. We expect annual dividend hikes of 2% to 2.5% in coming years.

Figure 9-23. SCANA Corp. (SCG)

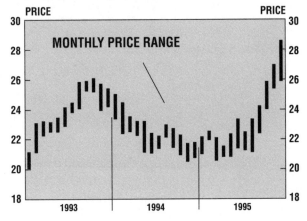

Southern Co.

270 Peachtree St. N. W.
Atlanta, GA 30303
(770) 393-0650

SO/New York Stock Exchange
Dividends paid since 1948
S&P earnings and dividend ranking: A−
Indicated annual dividend as of December 31, 1995: $1.22
Increase in dividends from 1985 to 1995: 14%
$1,000 invested on 12/31/1985 worth on 12/31/1995 with
dividends reinvested: $4,362
Ten-year annualized total return: 15.9%
A dividend reinvestment plan is available.

A low-cost power producer with healthy finances, Southern Co. benefits from strong growth in the Atlanta area. Through subsidiaries, the company serves 3.4 million customers throughout the southeast. Electricity demand should grow 4% to 5% annually for several years in the company's service territory, which includes a new Mercedes Benz plant in Alabama.

To boost its returns, SO recently bought South Western Electricity plc, one of twelve electric distribution companies in the United Kingdom, for $1.8 billion. Despite the cost, South Western should make a modest contribution to profits in 1996. The company also has development projects in Latin America.

Back in the U.S., Southern's base is about 27% industrial, but the utility faces little danger of losing these customers to competitors because its rates are below average for power companies. From 1996 through 1998, the company estimates that capital outlays for construction projects will total approximately $4.2 billion. Projects include construction of combustion turbine units to add about 600 megawatts of peak capacity by 1998. In addition, the company plans to upgrade existing generating plants to extend their useful lives.

Dividend growth is likely to be above the industry average over the next several years.

Figure 9-24. Southern Co. (SO)

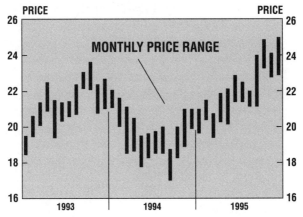

Where to Find
Helpful Information

Information from many of the following sources can be found at larger public libraries. In addition, full-service brokers will be happy to provide you with earnings estimates or data on a company's recent dividend history. If you deal with a discount broker, you may have to pay a small fee for reports that cover these items.

Basic Company Information

Public companies must file a great deal of information with the **Securities and Exchange Commission (SEC)**. If you have a computer with a modem and browser software, you can access company filings through EDGAR, the SEC's online service at: **http://www.sec.gov.**

If you don't have a computer, or would prefer to deal with a print version of the information, contact the investor relations department of the company you want to know about. Request the latest annual report, 10-K report (issued annually, it's more detailed and more valuable than the regular annual) and most recent 10-Q report (a quarterly). For addresses or phone numbers of companies, contact the exchange or market on which the firm's stock trades.

The American Stock Exchange Fact Book has addresses and phone numbers of all ASE-listed issues. Send a check or money order for $20 (New York State residents: $21.65, including sales tax) to:

Publications Dept.
American Stock Exchange
86 Trinity Place
New York, NY 10006

You can call the ASE with a request for a listed company's address and phone number at **(212) 306-1490.** Computer users may obtain the information from the American Stock Exchange's website: **http://www.amex.com.**

The National Association of Securities Dealers (NASD), which operates the Nasdaq market (known to older investors as the over-the-counter market), also has a **Fact Book** that lists company addresses and phone numbers. The $20 book is available from NASD Media-Source. Credit card holders call **(301)-590-6578.** NASD will handle phone inquiries for addresses and phone numbers of Nasdaq-traded companies. Call the market research department at **202-728-8015.** Or you can access NASD's website at **http://nasdaq.com.**

The New York Stock Exchange's research department will provide you with phone numbers of up to five NYSE-listed companies at no charge. Call the NYSE at **(212) 656-3218.**

Consensus Earnings Estimates

First Call has earnings estimates for about 5,500 U.S. companies, available online, by fax, or in print. The print version, **First Call Consensus Estimate Guide,** is a monthly publication that sells for $250 a year. Single copy is $50. Call **800-448-2348.** The estimates are sold through a **fax-on-demand** service. Prices vary, but you can obtain a free sample by calling **800-418-3333** using a touch-tone phone. First Call estimates are also available through **America Online.**

I/B/E/S offers consensus estimates on more than 5,000 U.S. companies. Via **CompuServe,** I/B/E/S estimates are $0.50 each or $2.50 for a more detailed report. The I/B/E/S estimates are also available by telephone for $2 per minute. **Call 900-225-2622.** Online access to I/B/E/S is at **http://www.networth@galt.com.**

Standard & Poor's Earnings Guide is a monthly publication listing consensus earnings estimates for more than 4,300 companies. Annual subscription is $147. Call **800-221-5277.**

Dividend, Earnings, and Share Price Histories

Standard & Poor's Stock Reports provide a detailed look at any of 4,300 stocks. Touch-tone phone users may obtain reports by **fax or mail.** A basic two-page Stock Report is $6 and quantity discounts are available. For a free sample, call **800-826-7078.** Stock Reports are also sold via S&P's website: **http://www.stockinfo.standardpoor.com.**

The Value Line Investment Survey is a weekly publication providing data on 1,700 stocks. A full year's subscription is $570; a 10-week trial is $55. Call **800-833-0046.**

Dividend Aristocrats

Higher Annual Dividend for at Least 25 Years

Each of the companies in this table has paid its shareholders a higher dividend every year for at least a quarter century. This is not a complete list, just a representative sample.

Table B-1

Company/Ticker	Industry	Number of Years Paid Higher Div.
Alco Standard/ASN	Business Products	30
American Brands/AMB	Diversified	28
American Business Products/ABP	Business Products	38
American Home Products/AHP	Health Care	44
Betz Laboratories/BTL	Chemicals	30

Table B-1 *(cont'd)*

Company/Ticker	Industry	Number of Years Paid Higher Div.
CCB Financial/CCBF	Financial Services	31
Central & South West/CSR	Utilities	44
Coca-Cola Co./KO	Food/Beverage	33
Commerce Bancshares/CBSH	Financial Services	27
Emerson Electric/EMR	Electrical Equipment	39
Frontier Corp./FRO	Telecommunications	36
H.J. Heinz/HNZ	Food/Beverage	28
Harcourt General/H	Diversified	27
Hartford Steam Boiler Insurance/HSB	Financial Services	30
Hormel Foods/HRL	Food/Beverage	29
International Flavors & Fragrances/IFF	Chemicals	35
Johnson & Johnson/JNJ	Health Care	33
Kellogg Co./K	Food/Beverage	39
Lilly (Eli)/LLY	Health Care	27
Mark Twain Bancshares/ MTWN	Financial Services	30
Marsh & McLennan Cos./MMC	Financial Services	32
Masco Corp./MAS	Building Products	37
Ohio Casualty/OCAS	Financial Services	49
Pfizer, Inc./PFE	Health Care	28
Procter & Gamble/PG	Household Products	40
Providian Corp./PVN	Financial Services	25
Rubbermaid, Inc./RBD	Household Products	44
Southtrust Corp./SOTR	Financial Services	26
Tambrands, Inc./TMB	Personal Products	44
Torchmark/TMK	Financial Services	45
U.S. Bancorp/USBC	Financial Services	38

How to Be a Dividend Rich Investor

Given a choice between a high current dividend and a low growing one, you should always choose the latter. We'd like to leave you with a simple chart (on the next page) that shows you why. Let's say Tom's $100 nest egg returns a steady $6 annually. Jerry's $100 is invested in a stock that pays only $3 a year, but the company increases its dividend 10% annually. In the early years, Tom is clearly ahead. But by year nine Jerry's annual return has outpaced Tom's and will continue to grow as compounding continues.

Figure C-1

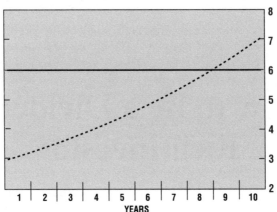

Index

About the Authors

Joseph Tigue is Managing Editor of Standard & Poor's investment advisory newsletter, *The Outlook*, as well as Editor of S&P's *Directory of Dividend Reinvestment Plans*. Mr. Tigue's frequent appearances in the business media include NBC, CNBC, CNN, PBS, the BBC, and various radio shows. He lives in Westbury, New York.

Joseph Lisanti is Senior Editor of Standard & Poor's *The Outlook*. Prior to joining S&P in 1989, Mr. Lisanti was Senior Editor of *Physician's Financial News* and Managing Editor of *Fact: The Money Management Magazine*. He lives in New York City and Great Barrington, Massachusetts.

Which Stocks Will Be Tomorrow's STARS?

Drawing on the vast experience of Standard & Poor's renowned staff of equities researchers and analysts, **The OUTLOOK** identifies the developments that affect stock performance — and makes recommendations on when to buy, hold, and sell. The outstanding features include:

- *Market Forecast and Investment Policy* — a weekly forecast of where the market is headed, and what moves you should make.

- *Supervised Master List of Recommended Issues* — Standard & Poor's favorites for long-term capital appreciation and for superior long-term total return, plus the new MidCap and SmallCap Master Lists.

- *Plus STARS — One of Standard & Poor's Most Powerful Investment Decision-Making Tools!* The highly regarded *Stock Appreciation Ranking System* offers an easy way to pick stocks that Standard & Poor's believes will do best in the near term — six months to one year. Week after week, STARS ranks 1,100 active stocks from One- to Five STARS, so you can track changes at a glance.

MAIL COUPON TODAY FOR A FREE ONE-MONTH SUBSCRIPTION!

Standard & Poor's The OUTLOOK

Please enter my FREE one-month subscription (four issues) to **The OUTLOOK** — Standard & Poor's premier weekly investment advisory newsletter — bringing me the best guidance on Wall Street and specific stock recommendations from the experts in the field.

NAME

ADDRESS

CITY/STATE/ZIP

TELEPHONE

Orders accepted on this original form only. Copies of this form will not be accepted.
Bill and Term = 7   Installation = D

Fill-in now and mail to: **Standard & Poor's**

A Division of The McGraw-Hill Companies
25 Broadway, New York, NY 10004   CJTR TPJ-096